AERODATA INTERNATIONAL

U.S. Navy Carrier Bombers Of World War II

TBD Devastator • SBD Dauntless
SB2C Helldiver • TBF/TBM Avenger

squadron/signal publications

Published 1987 by Squadron/Signal Publications, Inc.
1115 Crowley Drive
Carrollton, Texas 75011-5010

ISBN 0-89747-195-4

Printed in Hong Kong
for Imago Productions (F.E.) Pte. Ltd.

DOUGLAS TBD DEVASTATOR

Fig. 1   VT-2 in full regalia. The squadron leader's aircraft, '2-T-1' sports a full red cowling and fuselage stripe indicating that it is also first section leader. The 'E' was awarded for excellence in Individual Battle Practice, a much sought after honour carried by three TBDs in this view. All wing uppersurfaces are chrome yellow with red chevrons and black wingwalks. (NASM)

The Douglas TBD-1 Devastator has gone down in history as a failure. Its critics point to slow speed, lack of range and limited payload as all contributing to its downfall. So completely was it overwhelmed at the Battle of Midway that of 41 Devastators to attack the Japanese fleet that day, only five returned. One squadron, the ill-fated VT-8, was totally destroyed, every one of its 15 TBDs falling to a combination of effective anti-aircraft fire and hovering Zeros. Yet, to be fair to the Devastator, it should not have even been there and, had the Japanese delayed their plans for even a few months, it would not have been. BuAer knew full well that the TBD was obsolete. Indeed, its successor was already on the production lines and the first examples, ironically in the colours of VT-8, had just arrived in time to be bloodied at that same battle. Like the Brewster Buffalo, whose history is at least superficially similar to the Devastator's, the TBD has been branded a failure when really its only fault was being old.

This is not to say that the TBD-1 was a brilliant design, because it most certainly was not. Still, the end of the Devastator's story is so inglorious that it is easy to forget that the TBD had once been revolutionary in its innovation, setting the pattern for all that came after. Its list of firsts is impressive. The TBD was the first all-metal aircraft and the first monoplane ordered by the US Navy for carrier service and the first with power wing folding. It should be remembered that at the time of the Devastator's introduction, the standard US Navy carrier fighters were biplanes (F2Fs, F3Fs & F4Bs), not being replaced by monoplanes for two-and-a-half years. Further, it preceded its admittedly superior Japanese counterpart into the air by almost two years. Before too harsh a judgement is made, the Devastator's age and the incredibly rapid pace of aircraft development in the late 1930s must be taken into consideration.

The Devastator's design originated with a Request for Proposals by BuAer on 30 June 1934. The Navy needed a new torpedo and level bomber to replace its ageing biplane Martin BM-1s and Great Lakes TG-2s. The request was very general, leaving considerable latitude to the submitting firms. Only three companies responded and only two proposals were given serious consideration (one response, from Hall, was for a high-wing seaplane which failed to meet the carrier suitability requirement). The Great Lakes proposal for a three-place biplane and Douglas' for an all-metal monoplane were accepted and each firm was ordered to build a single prototype. In the event, the Great Lakes XTBG-1 proved to handle poorly and exhibit considerable instability in the air, clearing the way for the Douglas XTBD-1.

Fig. 2 The TBD mockup, beautifully constructed of plywood and canvas, even sporting a real Twin Wasp, is seen at Santa Monica on 24 April 1934. Note the auxiliary .30in (7.62mm) machine gun external mounting under the cockpit. (USN/NARS)

Fig. 3 Pre-war mockups were exact reproductions of the finished product, showing off not only the external form but all the framing as well. Everything is neatly labelled, down to the oil cooler, starter crank socket, retractable step and a pair of plywood and canvas 500lb bombs. (USN/NARS)

Fig. 4 *The XTBD-1 in its original configuration. Note the long, low canopy and the oil cooler located under the cowling. Also note the pair of 500lb bombs slung under the fuselage. (USN/NARS)*

Fig. 5 *After a visit to Santa Monica in late 1935, the prototype emerged with a higher canopy and small oil cooler intakes on either side of the cowling replacing the single ventral scoop, 4 November 1936. (USN/NARS)*

For its time, the Devastator was an advanced aircraft. All-metal, except for fabric-covered control surfaces, the XTBD-1 looked sleek and swift in comparison with its contemporaries. A long, low "greenhouse" fully enclosed positions for pilot, bombardier and radio operator/gunner. A pair of small doors in belly in front of the wing opened to provide visibility for the bombardier for level bombing. All payload was to be carried externally, a torpedo would fit into a semi-recessed position under the belly, bombs would be carried on two permanent shackles between the landing gear and on removable shackles which could be fitted outboard. (With a torpedo in position, the bomb-aiming doors would still open but all visibility would be blocked by the torpedo's warhead. For torpedo attack, aiming was done by the pilot through his gunsight. Generally, for torpedo attacks, the bombardier was left back on the carrier and the TBD was flown with a crew of two.) The Devastator's landing gear retracted rearward into partial recesses. A noticeable feature was the use of corrugated skinning on the wing outer panels.

Power was provided by a Pratt & Whitney XR-1830-60 Twin Wasp, a two-row, 14-cylinder, air-cooled radial offering 800hp for takeoff. Maximum speed was just under 200mph (322km/hr) at 8000ft (2438m). Cruising speed was 120mph (193km/hr) with normal load, only 100mph (161km/hr) with a big Mk 13 torpedo hanging down. Range was 435 miles (700km) with torpedo and 700 miles (1127km) without. Maximum load was a single torpedo or an equivalent 1200lb (544kg) of bombs. By the standards of five years later, the Devastator was slow, short-ranged and under-powered, but it represented a considerable step up from the biplanes it was designed to replace, and thus pleased BuAer. (At the same time that Devastators were entering the fleet, another new type, the Curtiss SBC-3 was also seeing first squadron service. The Curtiss was a biplane which had started life as a monoplane! It was faster and generally more satisfactory than the TBD-1 but, ironically, all SBCs had been replaced by the more modern SBD by the time of Pearl Harbor, while Devastators soldiered on to disaster.)

The XTBD-1, BuNo 9720, first flew on 15 April 1935. After very brief manufacturer's trials, which indicated no serious handling problems, it reported to NAS Anacostia, DC, for the first in a long series of Navy tests. Performance trials at Anacostia started in late April and ran through May. Night flying tests at NAS Norfolk took up June and bombing tests at NPG (Naval Proving Grounds) Dahlgren, VA, continued through all of July and August and half of September. Torpedo trials at Norfolk in September and October led up to the critical carrier suitability tests which took place on *Lexington* off San Diego from 5–10 December 1935.

The Navy pronounced itself satisfied with its new bomber. The only change made during a return visit by the prototype to its Santa Monica, CA, birthplace was the replacement of its low canopy by a considerably taller one, in response to pilot's complaints about visibility. On 3 February 1936, the Navy ordered 114 TBD-1s from Douglas, BuNo 0268-0381. 15 more were added on at a later date, BuNo 1505–1519, bringing total Devastator orders to 129, a large order considering the date.

Fig. 6   A close-up of the port side of the XTBD-1 showing the new canopy. The finish is overall aluminium paint with black wingwalks. (Douglas from Harry Gann)

*Fig. 7 **The first production Devastator, BuNo 0268, is seen on 28 June 1937. Note the revised cowling and relocated oil cooler intake.** (NASM)*

The differences between the first production Devastator and the prototype were relatively few. A 900hp R-1830-64 replaced the lower powered -60, but changes in performance were minimal. Maximum speed now hit 206mph (332km/hr) at 8000ft (2438m) and cruising speed unladen rose slightly to 125mph (201km/hr). Any significant performance increase would have required a bigger engine than was then available. Other changes involved a redesign of the cowling to fair its lower edge more smoothly into the fuselage, the movement of the oil cooler from below the cowling to the leading edge of the starboard wing and the addition of two machine guns. A fixed .50 (12.7mm) machine gun was set into the nose, firing through the starboard side of the cowling, and a flexibly-mounted .30 (7.62mm) machine gun was provided for the radio

operator/gunner which, when not in use, fitted neatly into a flap-covered trough aft of the gunner's position.

The first production TBD-1, BuNo 0268, led an interesting life. Reserved for test purposes during the early days after its delivery in July 1937, it was chosen to become the only TBD-1A (the only Devastator variant!), a float version of the bomber, in mid-1939. Given a pair of steerable Edo floats on 14 August, 0268 began water testing at Newport, RI, on 28 September. While no adverse effects resulted from the modification, apart from further loss of speed, interest in offensive floatplanes in the US never got much beyond the experimental stage. The first Devastator underwent intermittent testing as a floatplane through 1943 before being written off.

*Fig. 8 **In its final incarnation, 0268 became the sole XTBD-1A floatplane, seen here at the ramp, NAS Anacostia.** (Douglas from Harry Gann)*

Figs. 9 & 10 The Devastator production line at Santa Monica, 7 January 1938. Of interest is how early in the production process all markings were applied, including the squadron, section and individual aircraft designators and tails in air group colours, even squadron insignia. These aircraft are destined for Lexington's VT-2, hence the lemon yellow tail. Note the open bomb-aiming doors.
(Douglas from Harry Gann)

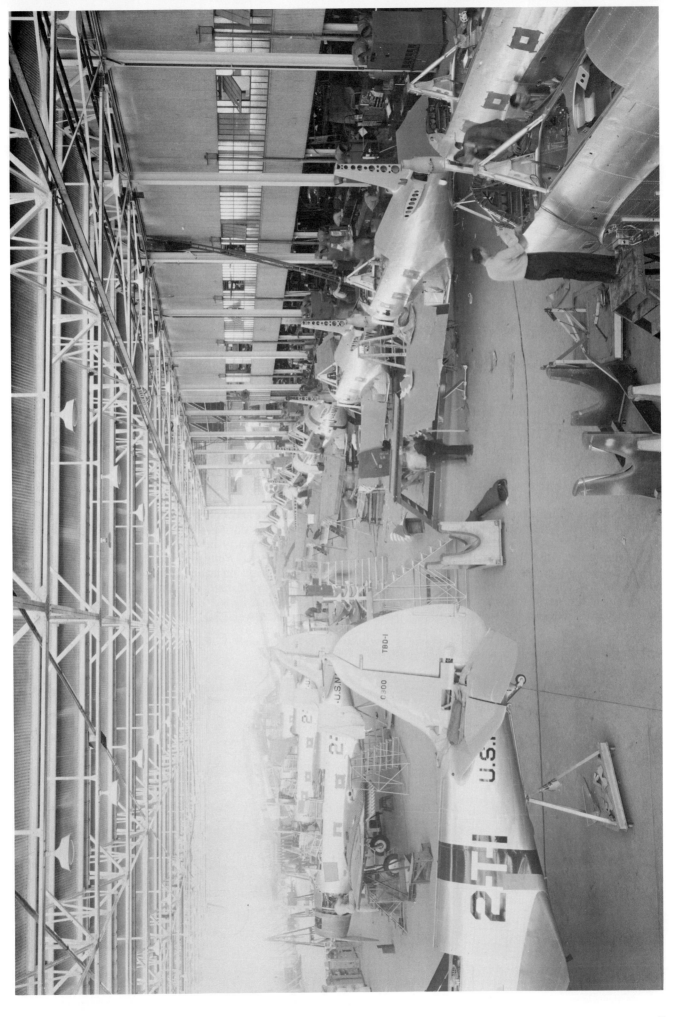

Fig. 11   '2-T-15' is seen during landing gear tests at Santa Monica, 19 January 1938. (USN/NARS)

Inevitably, comparisons with the Devastator's chief rival, the Nakajima B5N1 "Kate", crop up. (It should be always remembered that there was one more contemporary, the RN's Fairey Swordfish, which with a top speed of 139mph (224km/hr) made the Devastator look very good in comparison.) The Kate first flew in January 1937. Powered by a 770hp Nakajima Hikari 3 nine-cylinder radial, it could achieve a top speed of 230mph (370km/hr), could carry a payload of 1764lb (800kg) and could easily double the Devastator's range at 1400 miles (2253km). It should not be forgotten, however, that JNAF aircraft in general were built to lighter structural standards than their American contemporaries. The Japanese consistently placed range and manoeuvrability at a higher priority than pilot or airframe survivability. While the Devastator could not compare to later US designs in toughness (it lacked self-sealing fuel tanks and crew armour), it pointed the way toward those designs with its heavy construction.

The first squadron to switch over to Devastators was VT-3 off *Saratoga*, which traded in its TG-2s in November 1937. The other three carrier-based VTs followed suit as rapidly as TBD-1s became available. In the first half of 1938, *Yorktown*'s VT-5, *Lexington*'s VT-2 and the new *Enterprise*'s VT-6 all worked up their Devastators. Between then and December 1941, the TBD squadrons followed the routine of a peacetime navy, training and preparing for the war that everyone knew was coming. By that time, three other squadrons were operating or training in Devastators. The Navy's two smaller carriers, *Wasp* and *Ranger*, both operated a few TBD-1s during 1941. *Wasp*'s VS-71 acquired four Devastators early in the year and still had three when war broke out. *Ranger*'s VS-42 had three in May 1941 but had given them up again by year's end. One new fleet carrier, *Hornet*, was completing at the time of Pearl Harbor, and its VT-8 traded in its antique SBN-1s for not much newer TBD-1s at the time of the Japanese raid.

*Fig. 12   VT-3 was **Saratoga**'s torpedo squadron, indicated by the white tail. As the third aircraft in the third three-plane section, '3-T-9' has the lower half of its cowling in the section colour, true blue, 28 October 1937. (NASM)*

Fig. 13   Another VT-3 TBD, probably '3-T-10' (the full cowling and fuselage stripe indicate a section leader), the stripes therefore probably black. The stripe on the white tail is a landing assistance stripe, used by the LSO to help judge an aircraft's angle of approach. (Douglas from Harry Gann)

Fig. 14   '5-T-7' was third section leader of Yorktown's VT-5. The stripes are true blue, the tail red. Note the much fancier version of the 'E' and the abbreviated white landing assistance stripe extending only over tail's leading edge (the only part the LSO could actually see anyway), 16 November 1939. (USN/NARS)

Fig. 15   The last pre-war VT was Enterprise's VT-6, whose CO's aircraft is seen here. The stripes are first section red, the tail true blue. (USN)

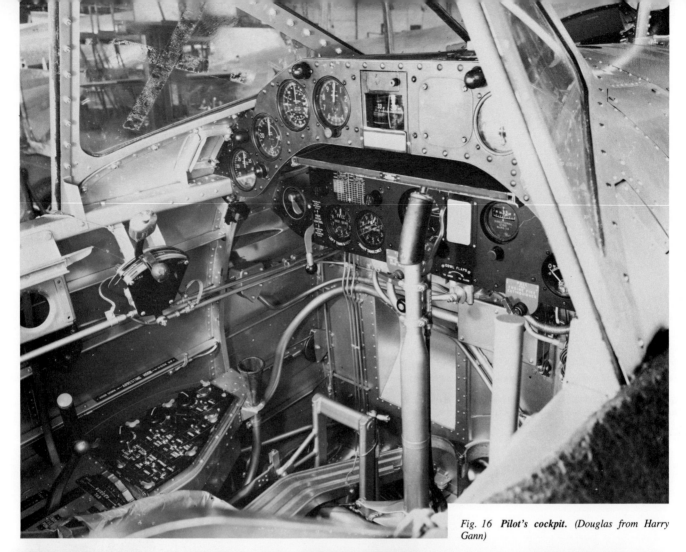

Fig. 16 **Pilot's cockpit.** *(Douglas from Harry Gann)*

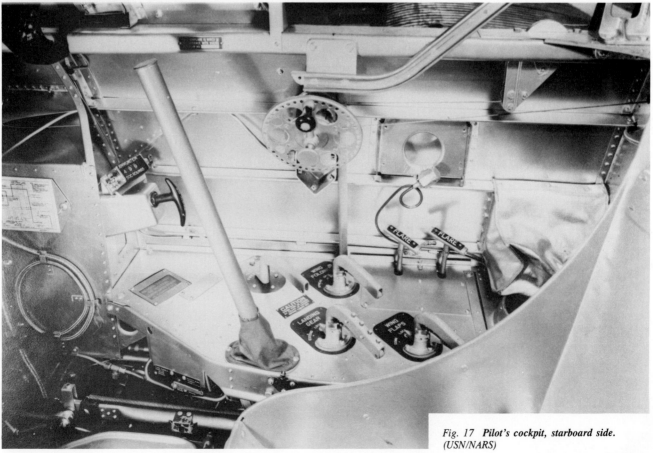

Fig. 17 **Pilot's cockpit, starboard side.** *(USN/NARS)*

Fig. 18 *Pilot's cockpit, port side. (USN/NARS)*

Fig. 19 *Cockpit floor showing bomb-aiming windows. (USN/NARS)*

Fig. 20 *Pilot's instrument panel.* *(NASM)*

Fig. 21 *Pilot's instrument panel seen from below.* *(USN/NARS)*

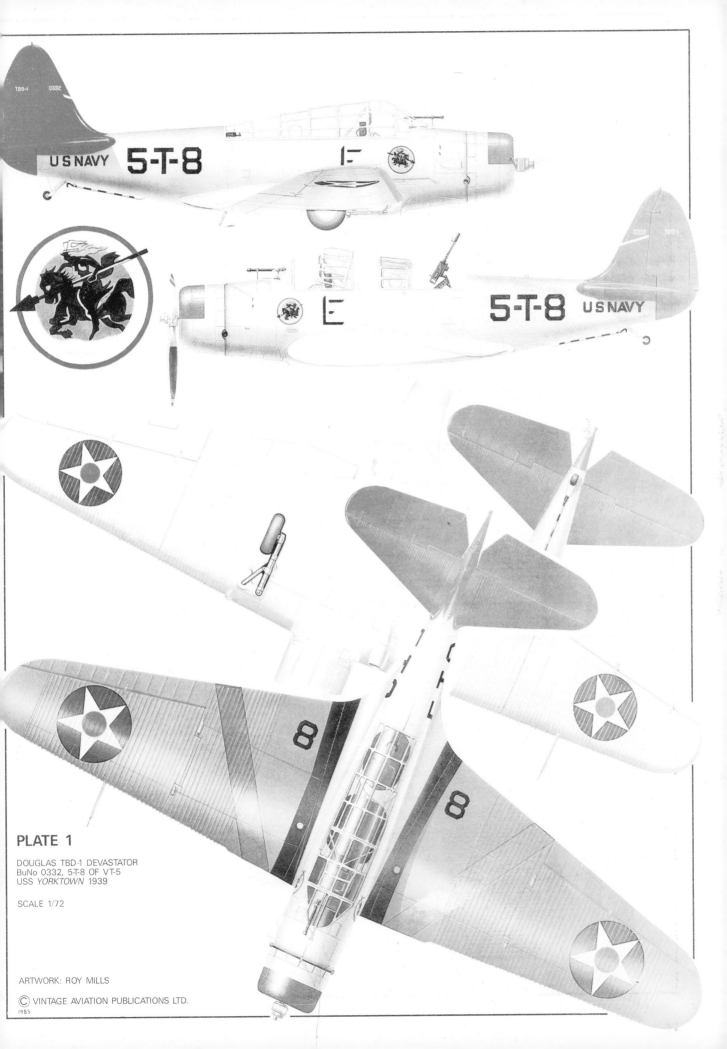

PLATE 1

DOUGLAS TBD-1 DEVASTATOR
BuNo 0332, 5-T-8 OF VT-5
USS *YORKTOWN* 1939

SCALE 1/72

ARTWORK: ROY MILLS

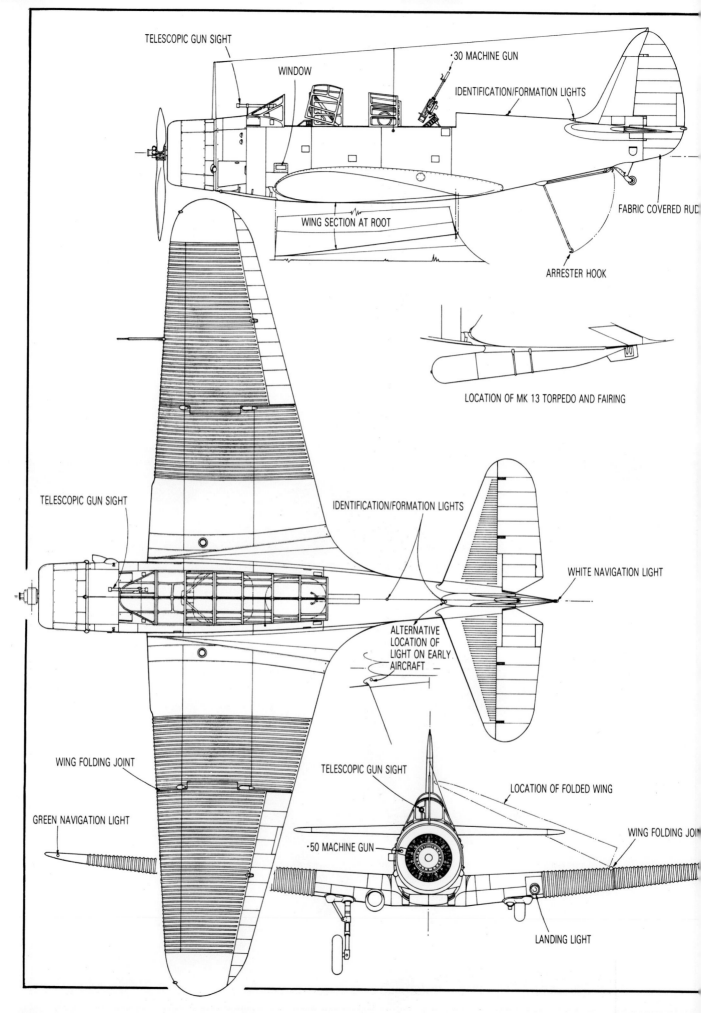

TELESCOPIC GUN SIGHT

WINDOW

·30 MACHINE GUN

IDENTIFICATION/FORMATION LIGHTS

FABRIC COVERED RUD

WING SECTION AT ROOT

ARRESTER HOOK

LOCATION OF MK 13 TORPEDO AND FAIRING

TELESCOPIC GUN SIGHT

IDENTIFICATION/FORMATION LIGHTS

WHITE NAVIGATION LIGHT

ALTERNATIVE
LOCATION OF
LIGHT ON EARLY
AIRCRAFT

WING FOLDING JOINT

TELESCOPIC GUN SIGHT

LOCATION OF FOLDED WING

GREEN NAVIGATION LIGHT

WING FOLDING JOI

·50 MACHINE GUN

LANDING LIGHT

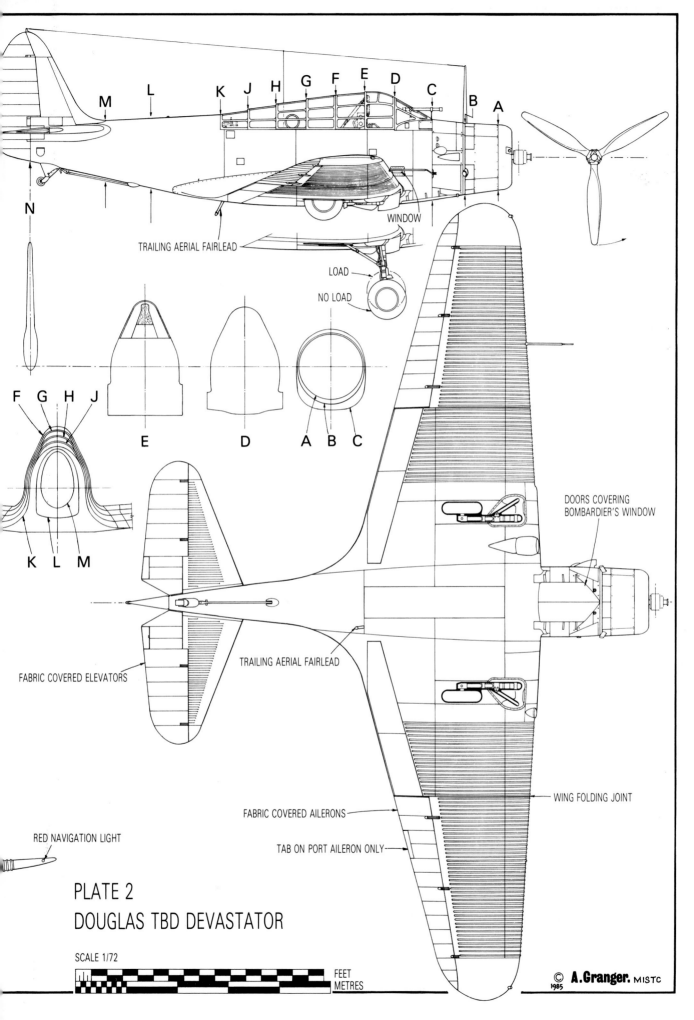

M L K J H G F E D C B A

N

WINDOW

TRAILING AERIAL FAIRLEAD

LOAD

NO LOAD

F G H J

E D A B C

K L M

DOORS COVERING
BOMBARDIER'S WINDOW

FABRIC COVERED ELEVATORS

TRAILING AERIAL FAIRLEAD

WING FOLDING JOINT

FABRIC COVERED AILERONS

TAB ON PORT AILERON ONLY

RED NAVIGATION LIGHT

PLATE 2
DOUGLAS TBD DEVASTATOR

SCALE 1/72

FEET
METRES

© A.Granger. MISTC
1985

15

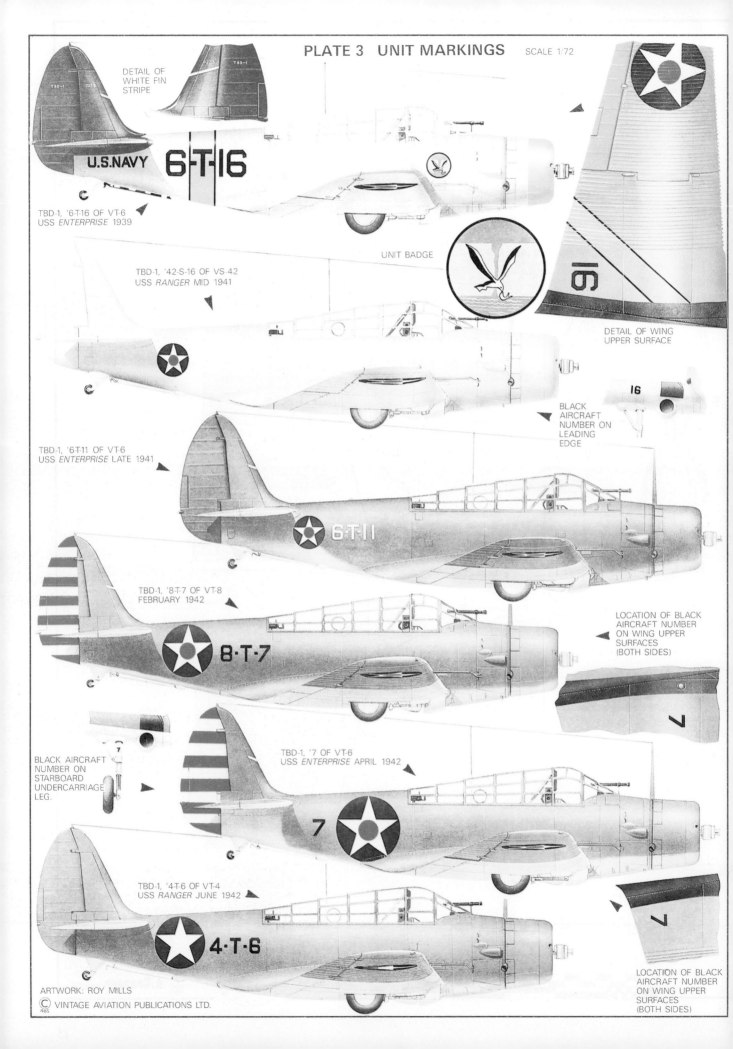

PLATE 3 UNIT MARKINGS

SCALE 1/72

DETAIL OF
WHITE FIN
STRIPE

U.S.NAVY 6·T·16

TBD-1, '6·T-16 OF VT-6
USS *ENTERPRISE* 1939

UNIT BADGE

TBD-1, '42-S-16 OF VS-42
USS *RANGER* MID 1941

DETAIL OF WING
UPPER SURFACE

BLACK
AIRCRAFT
NUMBER ON
LEADING
EDGE

TBD-1, '6·T-11 OF VT-6
USS *ENTERPRISE* LATE 1941

6·T·11

TBD-1, '8·T-7 OF VT-8
FEBRUARY 1942

LOCATION OF BLACK
AIRCRAFT NUMBER
ON WING UPPER
SURFACES
(BOTH SIDES)

8·T·7

BLACK AIRCRAFT
NUMBER ON
STARBOARD
UNDERCARRIAGE
LEG.

TBD-1, '7 OF VT-6
USS *ENTERPRISE* APRIL 1942

7

TBD-1, '4·T-6 OF VT-4
USS *RANGER* JUNE 1942

4·T·6

LOCATION OF BLACK
AIRCRAFT NUMBER
ON WING UPPER
SURFACES
(BOTH SIDES)

ARTWORK: ROY MILLS
© VINTAGE AVIATION PUBLICATIONS LTD.

Fig. 22   *The passing of the colourful pre-war markings came at the end of 1940, as the US Navy geared up for war. In its place was a basic camouflage of overall non-specular light gray. In October 1941, this was altered by having all surfaces visible from above painted non specular blue gray, as '6-T-11' here. This view dates from the brief period between then and January 1942 when red and white rudder stripes were ordered. (Douglas from Harry Gann)*

Fig. 23 VT-4 worked up on TBDs in February 1942, prior to service on board **Ranger** in the Atlantic. These aircraft also lack the rudder stripes which became mandatory on 5 January 1942. Units in the Atlantic often lagged far behind their Pacific counterparts in complying with markings regulations. (USN/NARS)

Fig. 24 '6-T-5' is seen in the air over Wake Island during the 'revenge raid' on 24 February 1942. With the outbreak of war, the squadron and mission designators were removed, leaving only the individual aircraft number. Enlarged roundels were ordered at the same time as the rudder stripes. (USN/NARS)

19

Figs.s 25 & 26 Two views of a TBD launching off Ranger near Bermuda, March 1942. '4-T-4' was marked in perfect October 1941 style, despite the late date of this view. (Note the absence of national insignia on the upper right and lower left wing surfaces. The January 1942 regulations ordered a return to four-position wing markings.) (USN/NARS)

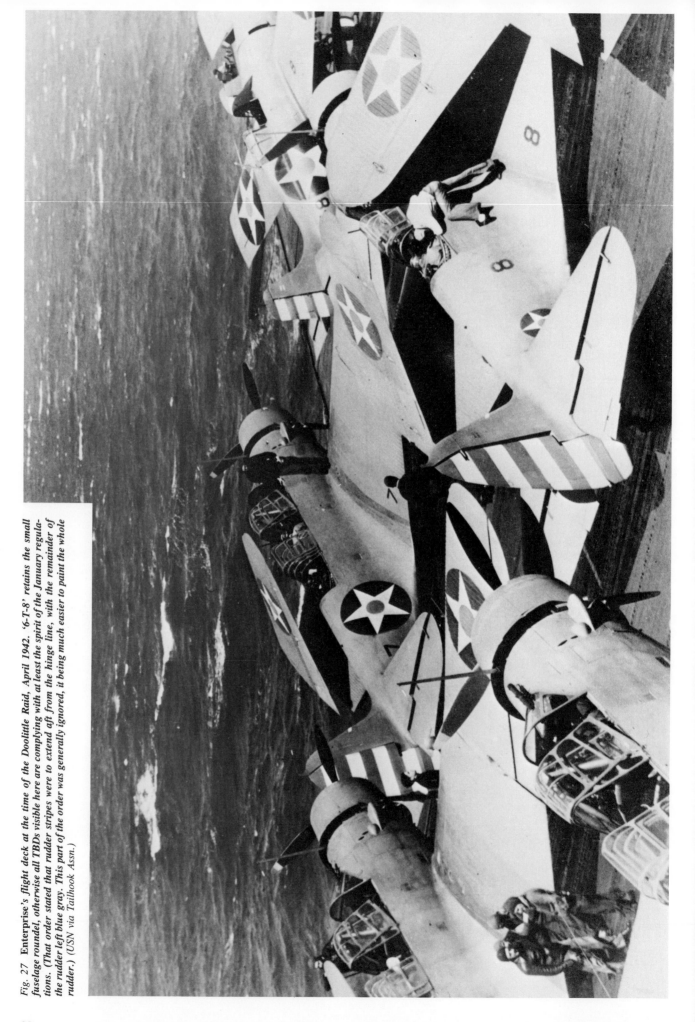

Fig. 27 Enterprise's flight deck at the time of the Doolittle Raid, April 1942. '6-T-8' retains the small fuselage roundel, otherwise all TBDs visible here are complying with at least the spirit of the January regulations. (That order stated that rudder stripes were to extend aft from the hinge line, with the remainder of the rudder left blue gray. This part of the order was generally ignored, it being much easier to paint the whole rudder.) (USN via Tailhook Assn.)

Fig. 28 *'6-T-5' gets its torpedo washed on* **Enterprise**, *11 April 1942. About a third of the MK 13 extended out of its recessed mounting. If torpedoes were left exposed to the elements for any length of time, it was general practice to wash them regularly to prevent corrosion. (USN/NARS)*

America had been extremely fortunate that 7 December 1941 found all three Pacific Fleet carriers (*Lexington*, *Saratoga* & *Enterprise*) not at home. Thus the nucleus of American naval force remained unscathed by the disaster that struck Pearl Harbor. Nevertheless, it took some time for the realisation to sink in that the loss of the battleline in the mud off Ford Island was not the end of the world. It did require the scrapping of Rainbow 5 (WPL-46), the prewar plan which called for a traditional slugging match between America's battleships and Japan's to decide the fate of the Pacific. Aircraft carriers had been assigned a relatively minor role in that plan: scouting, raiding and clearing the air of enemy aircraft, seeing to it that the American battleline arrived at the scene of the "big battle" (presumably somewhere in the Phillipine Sea) with as few losses as possible. Now suddenly the battleships were gone, and new plans had to be drawn. Somehow the entirely unexpected momentum of the initial Japanese thrusts had to be slowed, and someway had to be found to extract some measure of revenge for the humiliation of Pearl Harbor. Only aircraft carriers now remained to do the job.

Immediately, the carrier air groups went over to full war footing. In the VTs, this involved the removal of all flotation equipment from Devastators, so that the still-secret Norden bombsight that each one carried would sink. Strategically, it involved bringing *Yorktown* back from the Atlantic, in order to create a fourth carrier task force in the Pacific. To make up for the loss to the Atlantic Fleet of its only full-size carrier, both *Ranger*'s and *Wasp*'s air groups were upgraded. Two new squadrons were formed on Devastators, VT-4 for *Ranger* and VT-7 for *Wasp*. Unfortunately, the torpedoing of *Saratoga* by I-6 on 11 January 1942 made all this

effort vain, reducing the Pacific Fleet to three carriers again. Nevertheless, after the abortive relief of Wake and the successful reinforcement mission to Samoa in January 1942, the Pacific Fleet, now under Adm Nimitz, was ready for revenge.

The first of the "revenge raids" came on 1 February in the Gilberts. Launching from 36 miles (58 km) off Wotje Is., *Enterprise* Air Group hit Kwajelein and Roi. Nine TBD-1s of VT-6 attempted to attack shipping in the atoll, without much success. The main reason for this failure was the Mk 13 Bliss/Leavitt torpedo and not the Devastator. The standard American air-dropped torpedo was the best ally the Japanese could have wanted; it was inadequate in every respect and failed every comparison with its Japanese counterpart. The Mk 13 was fragile. It had to be dropped no higher than 120ft (37m), or it would break up on hitting the water (Kates often dropped successfully from 500ft (152m)). Even an "orange crate" plywood protector tried out at Kwajelein failed to strengthen the Mk 13. Likewise, Mk 13s had to be dropped at a speed no greater than 130kts (241km/hr), making the launching aircraft an easy target for fighters or gunners. Once in the water, the Mk 13's problems continued. Many would simply bury themselves in the mud or run erratically. And, if it survived these problems and actually ran towards a target, it still faced long odds. It was slow. With a single set speed of 33.5kts (62km/hr), it could be outrun by many of its targets (the Japanese Type 95 ran at 45kts (83km/hr) over a longer range). Further, the Mk 13 left a noticeable trail of bubbles while the Japanese did not, making it easier to spot and thus avoid. Even if a Mk 13 hit its target, there was no guarantee it would explode.

Fig. 29 Perhaps the last view of a VT-2 Devastator, this photo was taken on Lexington *about 1430 on 8 May 1942, as Air Group 2 was being recovered. About 15 minutes later, a major explosion tore through the ship, leading to her being abandoned and sunk later that afternoon. (USN/NARS)*

American torpedoes, through the first two years of the war, suffered a high percentage of exploder failures eventually traced to using too weak a firing pin (on impact it would crumple before it could strike the primer). And even if it exploded, it carried too small a warhead (500lb (227kg) vs. 900lb (408kg) for the Japanese) to assure serious damage. All of these factors added up to virtually guarantee failure for any aircraft doomed to carry such a weapon.

The Devastator's lack of success in that first "revenge raid", in retrospect, certainly can be understood, though at the time some rather exaggerated claims were made and believed. VT-6 claimed two transports sunk at Kwajelein and a further 10 transports and a single gunboat damaged. In fact, minor damage was achieved on one training cruiser (*Katori*), a minelayer and five transports. Only a small armed trawler was actually sunk. Later in the day, VT-6 sortied again, this time as horizontal bombers against the Japanese airfield on Taroa. Significant damage on base facilities was achieved, but the airfield remained operational. At least all of *Enterprise*'s Devastators returned. *Yorktown*'s VT-5 attacked Jaluit on the same day, running into bad weather enroute which broke up the attacking formations. Two TBDs collided in mid-air and two more ran low on fuel and landed on Jaluit, the crews spending the rest of the war as guests of the Japanese. Neither raid

brought results worthy of the risks or losses. The VTs knew that they were just marking time, waiting for a chance to get at their natural enemy, the Japanese carriers.

More raids followed, the results tending to be equally disappointing. *Enterprise* and VT-6 went after Wake on 24 February and Marcus Is. on 4 March. The last of the raids, a 10 March foray across New Guinea to attack Lae and Salamaua was the boldest and, in retrospect, the most foolish. *Lexington*'s and *Yorktown*'s air groups launched from 45 miles (72km) off the south coast near Port Moresby, crossed the 7500ft (2134m) passes of the Owen Stanley Range and achieved complete surprise on the two Japanese-held bases. Unfortunately, it was not worth the effort. 23 Mk 13s dropped by VT-2 and VT-5 actually achieved only one hit (a 6000GRT transport being sunk). Even had the torpedoes performed, the results would have been meagre. The largest target found was an old light cruiser. The futility of this raid, and the great potential risk in such long overland flights, finally brought the "revenge raids" to a close. Anyway, the cryptanalysts of ONI had pieced together the outline of a major Japanese naval thrust against Port Moresby and the Solomons. All available forces had to be mustered to meet the threat. The raids had not been a total waste, however. They did provide some valuable practice for the "big show" coming up.

Fig. 30 VT-8 before disaster struck. Seen during training in February 1942, '8-T-7' retains her full coding but otherwise has textbook markings, including a rare example of correctly applied rudder stripes. (USN/NARS)

Fig. 31 VT-6 prepares to launch on the morning of the Battle of Midway, 4 June 1942. Just barely visible are the markings changes that immediately preceded that battle, including removal of the rudder stripes. The red dot in the centre of the roundel was removed at the same time. (NASM)

Devastators are famous, or notorious, for their exploits in the Pacific, but they did visit other climes, perhaps the strangest and least known being the visit of VT-7 to Scapa Flow in spring 1942. In the continuing crisis in the Mediterranean, the Royal Navy had found itself critically short of aircraft carriers to transport fighters to Malta. An appeal to the US Navy brought *Wasp* to the eastern Atlantic in March. In order to clear the decks for Spitfires, *Wasp*'s TBDs were landed at Scapa, where they remained for nearly two months. Rather than remain idle, VT-7 kept itself busy flying anti-submarine patrols in the Denmark Strait and toward the coast of Norway.

If the Devastator was ever to have an ''hour'', it should have been at Coral Sea. Again, any success it could have achieved was negated by the woeful inadequacy of its torpedoes. The Coral Sea campaign began on 4 May 1942 with a raid by Air Group 5 on Tulagi, across the straits from Guadalcanal, where the Japanese had just set up a seaplane base. 22 Mk 13s dropped by VT-5 in the shallow harbour resulted in one hit. One old destroyer was sunk. Three days later, VT-5 along with VT-2 went after bigger game. Along with *Lexington*'s and *Yorktown*'s Dauntless squadrons, they found the

small carrier *Shoho* and dispatched her with ease. VT-2 claimed three hits and VT-5 claimed five, though in the confusion of nearly simultaneous bomb and torpedo attacks those claims were probably exaggerated. The real test came the next day, however, when the ''heavies'' took on each other. This time, the Devastator was found wanting. While Japanese torpedoes holed *Lexington* and contributed to her demise, the Devastators achieved no hits at all on the rapidly manoeuvring *Shokaku*, contributing to her survival.

The TBD's last show came barely a month later. The attrition of Devastators in daily flying as well as combat inevitably took its toll. Neither *Yorktown* nor *Enterprise* could muster a full squadron and the replacements simply did not exist. *Saratoga*'s VT-3, which had seen no action because of that carrier's torpedoing in January, was ordered to replace VT-5 on *Yorktown*, the latter's pilots returning to the mainland to work up in TBF-1s. VT-6 picked up what remained of *Yorktown*'s TBDs to make a complete squadron. *Hornet*'s fresh VT-8 brought the number of Devastators available to Frank Jack Fletcher on the morning of 4 June to 41. By the time the sun set on that fateful day, there weren't enough TBDs left to form a single squadron.

*Fig. 32 '4-T-2' launching off **Ranger** in June 1942. Its lack of rudder stripes is now 'legal'. Full coding is still retained, but at least the red dot has been removed from the national insignia. (USN)*

The story of that dramatic day is well known. Air groups from all three US carriers with 39 TBDs (two of *Yorktown*'s borrowed Devastators failed to start) launched against the massed carrier might of the Imperial Japanese Navy. The strike got separated and some units never found their targets. All three VTs found the Japanese carriers, though by this time they had lost their vital fighter escort. The results were predictable. Condemned by the limits of the Mk 13 to fly a low and slow run-in, they proved easy meat for the lightning quick Zeros of the CAP and the massed AA fire of the fleet. The courage of those VT pilots, who pressed home their suicidal attacks until every TBD had either been shot down or had launched its torpedo against the enemy, goes beyond the power of words to describe. Incredibly, the sacrifice was not in vain. Despite the almost complete extinction of all three VTs (VT-3 lost ten out of 12, VT-6 lost 11 out of 14 and VT-8 lost all 15), their attack was an essential ingredient in the wondrous chain of chance events that led to the devastation of the Japanese fleet that day. Because the Japanese carriers had to dodge the Devastators' "death ride", they were forced to delay the launching of the strikes poised on their decks. Because the CAP came down to sealevel to attack the Devastators, it was not in position minutes later when *Enterprise*'s and *Yorktown*'s Dauntlesses arrived on the scene. Able to attack unhindered against flight decks still jammed with loaded aircraft, the SBD's in five minutes destroyed the pride of the Japanese carrier fleet. If it had been fiction, the story would have been rejected as being too improbable.

Only the postscript remained to be written. Two TBDs got back to *Yorktown* while two of the three *Enterprise* survivors landed successfully. Fletcher's six remaining Devastators participated in the attacks on Mogami and Mikuma on 5 and 6 June, without notable success. The number of TBDs in the Pacific Fleet dropped to two the next day when *Yorktown* sank, taking the four TV-3 survivors with her. This ended the TBD's combat career. *Wasp*'s VT-7 switched to TBFs before being transferred to the Pacific. *Ranger*'s VT-4 operated Devastators in the Caribbean until August, when that unit was disbanded and its aircraft turned over to training units at Corpus Christi and Miami.

Midway has been rightly adjudged a turning point in the war in the Pacific, though it did not mark the demise of Japanese carrier aviation, as is often claimed. The Americans would find out in the Eastern Solomons and again at Santa Cruz that the Japanese still had offensive punch left. Devastators would not be there, however, their place taken finally by the new Grumman Avenger. The Avenger was in every respect a superior aircraft, but that is only to be expected, considering the relative newness of its design. Certainly no tears were shed over the passing of the Devastator from active duty. Still, one fact should be borne in mind when drawing any final conclusions about the antique TBD-1. Like the Devastators, Avengers had flown against the Japanese carriers that day at Midway. Six VT-8 TBFs, too late to join *Hornet*, had staged up to Sand Is. only days before the battle. Like the Devastators, they found themselves attacking the massed enemy carriers without the benefit of fighter cover. Like the Devastators, their Mk 13s failed them miserably, achieving no hits. And like the Devastators, they were decimated. Five out of six VT-8 Avengers failed to return.

Fig. 33 Shortly after this photo of VT-4 parked on Ranger's deck was taken on 12 June 1942, the squadron was landed, ending the TBD's service with the fleet. (USN/NARS)

SPECIFICATIONS

TBD-1

Dimensions: length, 35ft 0in (10668mm); height, 15ft 1in (4596mm) span, 50ft 0in (15240mm); wing area, 422sq ft (39.2sq m).

Weights: loaded weight, 9862lb (4473kg); empty weight, 6182lb (2804kg).

Performance: max speed at 8000ft (2438m), 206mph (332km/hr); cruise speed, 125mph (203km/hr); rate of climb, 720ft/min (219m/min); range, 700 miles (1127km).

Powerplant: Pratt & Whitney R-1830-64 Twin Wasp of 900hp takeoff power.

Armament: 1×.30 (7.62mm) machine gun; 1×.50 (12.7mm) machine gun; 1×Mk 13 torpedo or 1200lb (544kg) bombs.

DOUGLAS SBD DAUNTLESS

Fig. 1 One foot in the Wright Cyclone's exhaust pipe, a mechanic checks the oil level while an armourer, placidly seated on a 100lb (45kg) bomb, adjusts a fuse setting. The aircraft is B6, an SBD-3 of VB-3 on Enterprise, April 1942. (USN/NARS)

For one aircraft to descend directly from another, like the SBD Dauntless descended from the BT-1, is far from unique in aviation history. Even the fact that one of the most popular aircraft ever to fly, the SBD, was derived from a rather mediocre design has a number of precedents. What perhaps makes the story of the Dauntless's development unique is the fact that the Douglas Dauntless was derived from the Northrop BT-1, a situation brought about when Jack Northrop sold out his minority interest in Northrop Aviation to his partner, Donald Douglas, in January 1938 in order to set up a completely independent company of his own. (After Northrop's first company failed in the Depression and was bought out by United Aircraft, Douglas helped him set up a second company, retaining 51% of the stock. The company Northrop set up in 1938, the third to bear his name, is the current Northrop Corp.) In the deal, Douglas Aircraft acquired Northrop's El Segundo, CA, plant and with it the XBT-2, Northrop's intended upgrade of the BT-1. With nothing more than a change of paint, the XBT-2 became the XSBD-1, and the Dauntless was born. (The departure of Jack Northrop was not as traumatic as it could have been. While Northrop was a renowned and innovative designer, he had not had much to do directly with the design of the BT-1. That had been the responsibility of Ed Heinemann, who stayed on at El Segundo when Northrop left.)

Fig. 2 The Dauntless's design derived directly from the unsuccessful Northrop BT-1, which equipped only two squadrons and was replaced by other aircraft as soon as they became available. 5-B-18 was the 18th aircraft of Yorktown's VB-5. As third plane in the sixth section, the bottom of its cowling and wing chevron were lemon yellow. Tail was insignia red. (USN/NARS)

Fig. 3 The Marines got the SBD-1 because the navy did not want it. BuNo 1626 was one of the aircraft flown by VMB-2's CO. Markings were Navy style. Cowling, fuselage stripe and wing chevron were royal red to indicate first section leader. Vertical red, white and blue tail stripes were authorised for any unit that did not have some other tail marking. By this date, late 1940, their use was restricted almost entirely to the Marines. (Douglas)

Whatever the twists in its development history, the SBD inspired more loyalty in its pilots than perhaps any other aircraft in history. Long after a technically superior replacement was available, carrier air groups resisted all efforts to take away their Dauntlesses. The reason certainly had nothing to do with the performance of the "Barge" (also known as the "Clunk"). The SBD's speed, range and payload were all barely adequate at best at the time of its introduction, and by 1943 it was decidedly obsolete. Why, then, did pilots hate to see the last of their SBDs? The answer is simple; the Dauntless was an easy aircraft to fly. It was docile, stable and forgiving. Whatever else may be said pro or con about the SBD's replacement, the Curtiss SB2C Helldiver, those three adjectives have never been included. Certainly, the Helldiver was faster, stronger and more potent, but flying the SB2C was work in every sense of the word. Flying the SBD was pleasure pure and simple; a Sunday drive compared to a rush-hour commute. Such an aircraft is rare in the history of aviation, at least among warplanes, and the uncommon loyalty of its pilots perhaps easy enough to understand.

Fig. 4 VMB-1 was the second Marine unit to receive SBD-1s. Here the CO's aircraft (BuNo 1603) is seen in pre-war markings. Note the Marine crest just behind the wing. (Note also that this photo was taken with orthochromatic film which turns the red dark while that above was in panchromatic which shows red light. Except for the squadron number and BuNo, these two aircraft were identically marked.) (Douglas)

31

Fig. 5 The chief distinguishing feature of the SBD-2 was the reduced airscoop atop the cowling. They were issued to carrier units despite BuAer's opinion that they weren't combat-worthy. Those that were not lost at Pearl Harbor were replaced by -3s shortly after. (Douglas)

The Douglas Dauntless, therefore, can be said to have originated with a 1934 request for proposals from BuAer to which Douglas Aircraft did not respond. The Navy requested proposals for a new carrier-based scout-bomber, an aircraft capable of either divebombing or patrol missions. The request did not specify aircraft layout in any way (rare for a BuAer RFP). The only specific requirements were that a bomb displacement apparatus be used to clear the propeller and that dive brakes be fitted to restrict terminal dive velocity. Two companies responded with biplane designs which were rejected out of hand. Four firms (Brewster, Martin, Vought and Northrop) submitted monoplanes. Northrop was ordered to build one prototype of its design for flight test evaluation.

The XBT-1 (BuNo 9745) was developed directly from the Northrop Gamma mailplane by Heinemann. (In fact, the XBT-1 was far from the first Gamma-derivative to see military service. Northrop had supplied more than 200 larger but basically similar A-17s to the USAAC prior to beginning work on the XBT-1.) The prototype was a low-wing monoplane with a partially enclosed, rearward-retracting landing gear. It had a wingspan of 41ft 6in (12649mm) and was 31ft 6in (9601mm) long. The RFP had not called for wing-folding and the XBT-1's wing did not. In fact, the characteristically Northrop multicellular wing had an essentially spar-less structure and it would have been difficult, if not impossible, to devise a satisfactory folding system for it. (This wing design had been one of the great features of the early Northrop mailplanes, among the first all-metal aircraft ever built. It was tremendously strong and light —at the time of its introduction. When Donald Douglas began work on his new DC-series of commercial transports, he incorporated the Northrop wing in his first preliminary sketch. By the mid-1930s, however, the design had already been surpassed by improved, lighter-weight, spar-based designs. Nevertheless, it was retained unchanged throughout the SBD-series. The Dauntless's lack of wing-folding was to remain a problem throughout its career.) Powered by an 825hp Pratt & Whitney R-1535-94 Twin Wasp Jr, the XBT-1 had a top speed of 184kts (341km/hr) and a service ceiling of 22,500ft (6858m).

Almost from its first flight on 19 August 1935, the new Northrop bomber had problems. Severe buffetting when the split flap/dive brakes were opened was solved by the perforation of the flaps. The remaining problems were not as easily remedied. These included poor lateral stability at slow speeds, accompanied by a loss of rudder effectiveness, and a vicious tendency to torque roll if power was increased too suddenly on approach. Despite these major handling deficiencies, the XBT-1 was accepted without further modification after only 60 days of testing, an order being placed by the Navy for 54 BT-1s (BuNos 0590/0643) which were to be used to equip *Yorktown*'s VB-5 and *Enterprise*'s VB-6.

Had that BT-1 production contract not included authorisation for the XBT-2, the story would probably end here, because the Navy was thoroughly displeased with the BT-1. They got what they had ordered, an inadequately developed aircraft with some dangerous handling problems. Certainly, no more BT-1s would be required. The original contract, however, had specifically included money for the modification of one production BT-1 in an attempt to resolve the problems, resulting in the XBT-2 (BuNo 0627). Heinemann reasoned that many of the BT-1's problems stemmed from it being underpowered and began by substituting a 1000hp Wright XR-1820-32 Cyclone for the Twin Wasp Jr. A three-bladed, adjustable-pitch prop replaced the BT-1's two-bladed model. Flight testing of the up-powered XBT-2, which began on 25 April 1938, revealed some improvement but not enough. Therefore, with the Navy's reluctant blessing, Northrop flew the XBT-2 to NACA Langley for wind-tunnel testing. NACA recommended a number of changes including the adoption of a completely-retracting landing gear, the inclusion of fixed slots in the wing to improve aileron effectiveness at slow speeds and an enlarged tail and rudder for improved lateral stability. The result was a series of modifications which, over the course of six months, turned the XBT-2 into the prototype Dauntless. In all, 21 different tail configurations and a dozen aileron designs were tried out before a satisfactory combination was found. Even the canopy was altered, being increased in height to improve pilot visibility. The effort evidently paid off, because the XSBD-1 (as it was now called) not only solved the BT-1s handling problems but emerged as one of the best handling aircraft ever to fly. BuAer accepted the XSBD-1 in February 1939 and an order was placed for 144 SBD-1s on 8 April. (The order for the XSB2C-1 was placed just over a month later on 15 May.)

The first SBD-1 was delivered on 6 February 1940. Armament was a pair of .50 (12.7mm) machine guns with 360 rounds each in the forward fuselage, firing above the cowling through the propeller arc, the gun breeches extending into the cockpit. Aiming was through a simple 3X telescopic sight which doubled as a bombsight. The observer/radio operator had a single .30 (7.62mm) machine gun on a flexible mount with 600 rounds. When not in use, the gun could be stowed in a flap-covered tunnel along the top of the fuselage. The bomb cradle could handle anything from a 500lb (227kg) to a 1600lb (726kg) bomb, with a 1000lb (454kg) bomb being the preferred load. Single racks outboard of the landing gear legs could carry an additional 100lb (45kg) bomb or depth charge each. Despite this offensive weaponry, the SBD-1 lacked a number of features necessary to make it truly combat-worthy. The 210gal (795lt) of fuel was stored in four unprotected tanks in the fuselage and wing centre-section. This fuel capacity was considered inadequate, providing too short an operational radius (range with bomb load was just 860 miles (1384 km)). Further, the SBD-1 lacked self-sealing liners for its fuel tanks, cockpit floor armour or an armoured windscreen, all items considered essential for combat aircraft by BuAer. With a design change planned for the 58th example, the Navy elected to accept the first 57 as they were and do what it always did with aircraft that it did not want, give them to the Marines. VMB-2 began working up on SBD-1s at MCAS Quantico in late 1940, followed by VMB-1 in early 1941. These squadrons were renamed VMSB-232 and -132 early in 1941, at which time they were joined by VMSB-231. That squadron and VMSB-232 were transferred to Hawaii in October 1941. Between them, they had 27 SBD-1s based at MCAS Ewa on 7 December 1941, when 17 were destroyed and all of the remainder damaged during the raid on Pearl Harbor.

Those Marine SBD-1s, surprisingly, were not the first Dauntlesses lost to Japanese action in WW2. That ''honour'' went to SBD-2s of VS-6 and VB-6 off *Enterprise*. The 87 SBD-2s (the remainder of the original 144 aircraft order) differed from the -1 only in

Fig. 6 An SBD-3 in correct spring 1942 markings (a rare bird indeed!), lacking only the squadron coding, which should be black. This example lacks the composite fairing over its prop hub but is otherwise ready for delivery, 4 March 1942. (NASM)

Fig. 7 Flaps down, elevator up, prop leaving corkscrews in the humid air, B8 launches off Enterprise, *February 1942. Note the overly large wing roundels, they were supposed only to extend back to the aileron break. (USN)*

fuel capacity. The two 15gal (57lt) wing centre section tanks of the -1 were replaced by 65gal (246lt) tanks in the wing outer sections, raising total fuel capacity to 310gal (1174lt) and boosting bombing range to 1172 miles (1886km). The increased weight of fuel and of the autopilot that was installed because the extreme search ranges the SBD-2 could reach, tended to harm performance, forced the deletion of one of fixed machine guns. The -2 still lacked any protection for its fuel system or crew, but the fleet needed to get its new bomber into service and BuAer had to relent. SBD-2s had been assigned to VS-6 and VB-6 and to *Lexington*'s VB-2 by the time of the attack on Pearl Harbor.

Thirteen SBD-2s of VS-6 along with four from VB-6, led by CAG Cdr Howard Young, launched off *Enterprise* as that carrier approached Oahu at dawn on 7 December 1941. The *Enterprise* Group, under the command of Rear Adm Bill Halsey, was on war-footing. Launching at 0630, the 18 Dauntlesses were to fly search patterns east of the carrier force and then proceed to Ewa. (It was standard pre-war practise for a carrier to fly-off its air group as it entered port and for its aircraft to operate from a land base for whatever time the carrier spent in port.) They flew into a war. 6-B-3 went down at almost exactly 0800, becoming the first US aircraft lost in combat with the Japanese. Facing not only Zeroes but also ''friendly fire'', Young and others landed at Ford Island amid bursting AA fire. One ploughed up a pasture on Kauai. Another shot up a Zeke over Ewa and then collided with its victim, both crashing in flames. Still others ditched offshore. Surprisingly, nine survived in serviceable condition and were armed and sent after the Japanese task force after noon on the 7th, too late to catch the now-retiring *Nagumo*.

The first truly combat-worthy Dauntless was the SBD-3, of which 584 were produced. The -3 came into existence as a direct result of an order for 174 by the Aeronavale, although, in the event, France fell before the first delivery could be made and all reverted to the US Navy. The SBD-3 featured, finally, self-sealing fuel tanks (with capacity for 260gal (984lt)—all in the wings), 167lb (76kg) (of cockpit armour and a bullet-proof windscreen. Despite the obvious increase in weight caused by these modifications, BuAer decided to accept the reduced performance and reinstated the second fixed, forward-firing machine gun. In an attempt to save weight, alclad replaced dural as the aircraft's skin, an R-1820-52 replaced the similarly powered -32 and all flotation equipment was removed. The net weight increase was thus kept to only 501lb (23 kg) resulting in a 3mph (5km/hr) drop in top speed to 250mph (402km/hr).

As the first major production model, the SBD-3 rapidly equipped all carrier-borne VBs and VSs (replacing SOCs, SB2Us and SBCs as well as SBD-2s) and began to be released to VMSBs. At the time of the Battle of Coral Sea, VB and VS-5 off *Yorktown* and VB and VS-2 off *Lexington* were exclusively equipped with SBD-3s, though some of *Yorktown*'s Dauntlesses had arrived only on 4 May, just three days before the battle began. The Dauntless drew first blood on 7 May, when all four squadrons ganged up to overwhelm the virtually undefended Japanese light carrier *Shoho*, *Yorktown*'s squadrons being given most of the credit. VS-2's CO, Lcdr Robert Dixon gained instant immortality when he radioed back to *Lexington*: ''Scratch one flattop, Dixon to carrier, scratch one flattop!'' The victory was not totally unclouded, however, as perhaps the most serious problem to face the Dauntless as a divebomber came to light that day, inadequate cockpit ventilation. Seemingly insignificant, it had never caused any difficulties before because all practise divebombing missions had been flown in relatively temperate weather. Now, as the SBDs nosed over from 15,000ft (4572m) where it is cold and relatively dry, to the hot and humid tropical air at sea level, windscreens and gunsights fogged up. It was a problem that was never totally solved, even in later models, although emergency measures did alleviate it somewhat. Obviously, it introduced another complication to the already tricky art of divebombing. Despite this, 13 hits were obtained by the 53 SBDs, enough to sink the first Japanese carrier lost to American action. Only three Dauntlesses were lost. Never again would the victory be quite so one-sided.

Figs. 8 & 9 SBD-3s of VS-6 and VB-6 prepare to launch off Enterprise against Wake Island, February 1942. The two squadrons can be distinguished by the code letter and by different styles of landing assistance stripes on the tail. Enterprise's group was probably the only one to exactly follow BuAer's early 1942 directive to remove squadron codes but retain mission designators and aircraft numbers. (USN/NARS)

Fig. 10 Even the best handling aircraft ended up in the catwalk every once in a while. Pilots and deckcrew run to the aid of B4 of VB-3 (Saratoga's VB) on board Enterprise, en route to Tokyo for the Doolittle Raid, 11 April 1942. (USN/NARS)

Fig. 11 A deckload of SBD-3s warm up on Enterprise *early in the morning of 8 May 1942. In the background,* Lexington *strikes down the dawn search from the bow while lining up attack aircraft at her stern. This would be the day of the first great carrier vs. carrier battle and* Lexington's *last afloat.* (USN/NARS)

The next day, SBDs struck again, though not as decisively and at greater cost. 46 Dauntlesses were launched against the main Japanese carrier force. The weather now favoured the defender, scattered rain squalls occasionally hiding *Shokaku* or *Zuikaku* from view. Most of *Lexington*'s CVG-2 never found the Japanese fleet at all and *Yorktown*'s group found only *Shokaku* and gained only two hits, though those caused enough damage to keep her out of the Midway campaign. This time the Dauntlesses encountered a full-scale CAP, losing 13 of their number over the target. Even worse, they returned to find *Lexington* sinking and *Yorktown* damaged, temporarily neutralising US carrier strength in the South Pacific.

The SBD's greatest day was still to come, however, less than a month later at the Battle of Midway. The truth of the notion that history is made not necessarily by the great and good but by those ordinary folks who happen to be at the right place at the right time was never better proved than on 4 June 1942. On that day, a handful of SBD-3 Dauntlesses changed the course of the war in a fashion as dramatic and decisive as any novelist could concoct.

Seven SBD squadrons took part in the Battle of Midway, three of them with a singular lack of success. VMSB-241 attacked the Japanese fleet early on 4 June with 16 SBD-3s. Five near-misses were obtained on *Hiryu*, but fully half of the squadron fell to the defenders. Out of the six squadrons that launched off the US carriers, both of *Hornet*'s squadrons, VS and VB-8, missed the enemy completely. VS and VB-6, *Enterprise*'s squadrons led by CAG Lcdr Wade McClusky, had been flying alongside *Hornet*'s group and would have similarly missed the Japanese were it not for McClusky's instincts and luck. When the four squadrons reached the enemy's projected position and found only vacant ocean, *Hornet*'s group turned southeast towards Midway because that was the direction the Japanese had last been seen heading. It made sense, but it was wrong and, worse, it took *Hornet*'s SBDs away from their carrier. (All but two of *Hornet*'s SBDs reached Midway, but they were out of the battle.) McClusky turned northeast reasoning that *Nagumo* had probably sighted the US

carriers and would be heading towards them and, if he was wrong, at least he would be heading back towards *Enterprise*. He guessed right. At the same time that he turned his squadrons towards the Japanese, *Yorktown*'s VS-5 and VB-3 (borrowed from *Saratoga*) were approaching *Nagumo* from the opposite direction, having launched more than an hour and a half after McClusky with an updated contact report.

Rarely has luck (and it cannot be called anything else) brought so many crucial factors together at the same time. Only by luck did McClusky's Dauntlesses find the Japanese fleet at all. Even after having correctly surmised that the enemy was northeast of his location, he would have passed them to west but for the fact that one destroyer had lagged behind to depth charge an American submarine. Only by luck did they arrive over the Japanese fleet at the exact same moment as Max Leslie's *Yorktown* group. Only luck (and the heroic sacrifice of three torpedo squadrons) saw to it that the enemy CAP was at sea level and not high above the fleet. And most critically, it was luck that placed four squadrons of SBD-3s over the Japanese fleet at their last moment of greatest vulnerability, decks loaded with armed aircraft. The Dauntlesses dived even as the Japanese carriers were turning into the wind to launch a strike that could very well have altered the war in their favour. Seemingly if any one of those factors was altered by even a few minutes, the results of those dives might have been far less devastating. As it was, in five crucial minutes, three Japanese aircraft carriers were fatally damaged and the tide of the war changed decisively in America's favour.

There was more action that day. The surviving Japanese carrier, *Hiryu*, launched a strike which holed *Yorktown* and was then, in turn, fatally wounded by *Enterprise*'s Dauntlesses, now under the command of Lt W. Gallaher. There would be action for SBD-3s on other days as well. The Battles of the Eastern Solomons and Santa Cruz were to come later in 1942. Marines would also fly -3s extensively in the Solomons campaign, continually harrassing the ''Tokyo Express'' and often rendering it ineffective. Had it never flown again, however, its reputation would have been undiminished because of those five minutes in June.

Fig. 12 Pilot's instrument panel.
1. Compass.
2. Landing gear warning.
3. Rounds counters.

(USN/NARS)

Fig. 13 Pilot's cockpit, starboard forward.
1. Engine primer.
2. Starter meshing pull.
3. Carburettor air control.
4. Parking brake handle.
5. Electrical distribution panel.
6. Oil cooler scoop control.
7. Fuel gauge pumps.
8. Cockpit ventilator.

(USN/NARS)

Fig. 14 *Pilot's cockpit, port forward.*
1. *Ignition switch.*
2. *Cowling flap control lever.*
3. *Blower control.*
4. *Throttle.*
5. *Mixture control.*
6. *Propeller control.*
7. *Bomb release.*
8. *Bomb arming lever.*
9. *Arresting hook lever.*
10. *Landing gear position indicator.*

(USN/NARS)

Fig. 15 *Pilot's cockpit, starboard rear.*
1. *Landing gear selector handle.*
2. *Diving flap selector handle.*
3. *Landing flap selector handle.*
4. *Emergency hydraulic pump.*
5. *Engine-driven hydraulic pump.*
6. *Flotation system pull.*
7. *Flap position indicator.*

(USN/NARS)

Fig. 16 *Pilot's cockpit, port rear.*
1. *Fire extinguisher pull.*
2. *Tail wheel lock.*
3. *Elevator tab control.*
4. *Rudder tab control.*
5. *Aileron tab control.*
6. *Fuel tank selector valve.*
7. *Map case.*
8. *Wobble pump.*
9. *Flare releases.*

(USN/NARS)

41

Fig. 17 *Pilot's seat installation.*
1. *Seat adjustment lever.*
2. *Headrest release lever.*
3. *Emergency landing gear lowering valve.*
4. *Chartboard.*

(USN/NARS)

Fig. 18 *Hoisting sling in stowed position.*
1. *Pilot's headrest.*
2. *Emergency flotation pull.*
3. *Enclosure latch.*
4. *Hydraulic reservoir.*

(USN/NARS)

PLATE 1

DOUGLAS SBD-3 DAUNTLESS
'S4 of VS-6
USS *ENTERPRISE*
FEBRUARY 1942

SCALE 1/72

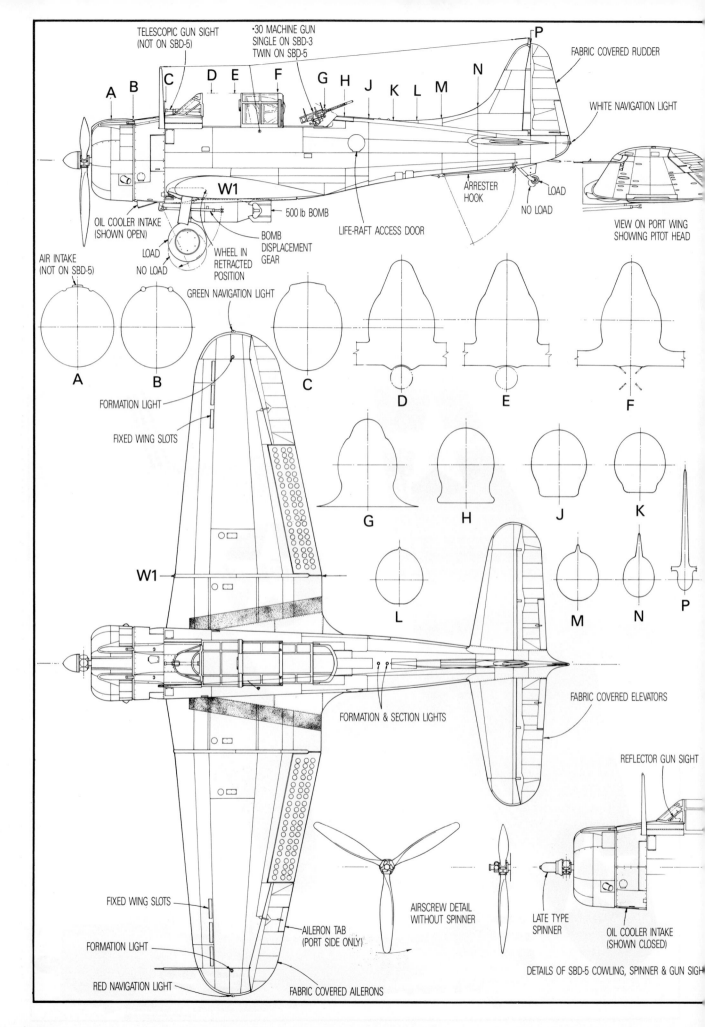

TELESCOPIC GUN SIGHT
(NOT ON SBD-5)

·30 MACHINE GUN
SINGLE ON SBD-3
TWIN ON SBD-5

P

FABRIC COVERED RUDDER

A B C D E F G H J K L M N

WHITE NAVIGATION LIGHT

VIEW ON PORT WING
SHOWING PITOT HEAD

ARRESTER
HOOK

LOAD

NO LOAD

OIL COOLER INTAKE
(SHOWN OPEN)

W1

500 lb BOMB

LIFE-RAFT ACCESS DOOR

LOAD

NO LOAD

BOMB
DISPLACEMENT
GEAR

WHEEL IN
RETRACTED
POSITION

AIR INTAKE
(NOT ON SBD-5)

GREEN NAVIGATION LIGHT

A   B   C   D   E   F

FORMATION LIGHT

FIXED WING SLOTS

G   H   J   K

W1

L   M   N   P

FABRIC COVERED ELEVATORS

FORMATION & SECTION LIGHTS

REFLECTOR GUN SIGHT

FIXED WING SLOTS

AILERON TAB
(PORT SIDE ONLY)

AIRSCREW DETAIL
WITHOUT SPINNER

LATE TYPE
SPINNER

OIL COOLER INTAKE
(SHOWN CLOSED)

FORMATION LIGHT

RED NAVIGATION LIGHT

FABRIC COVERED AILERONS

DETAILS OF SBD-5 COWLING, SPINNER & GUN SIGHT

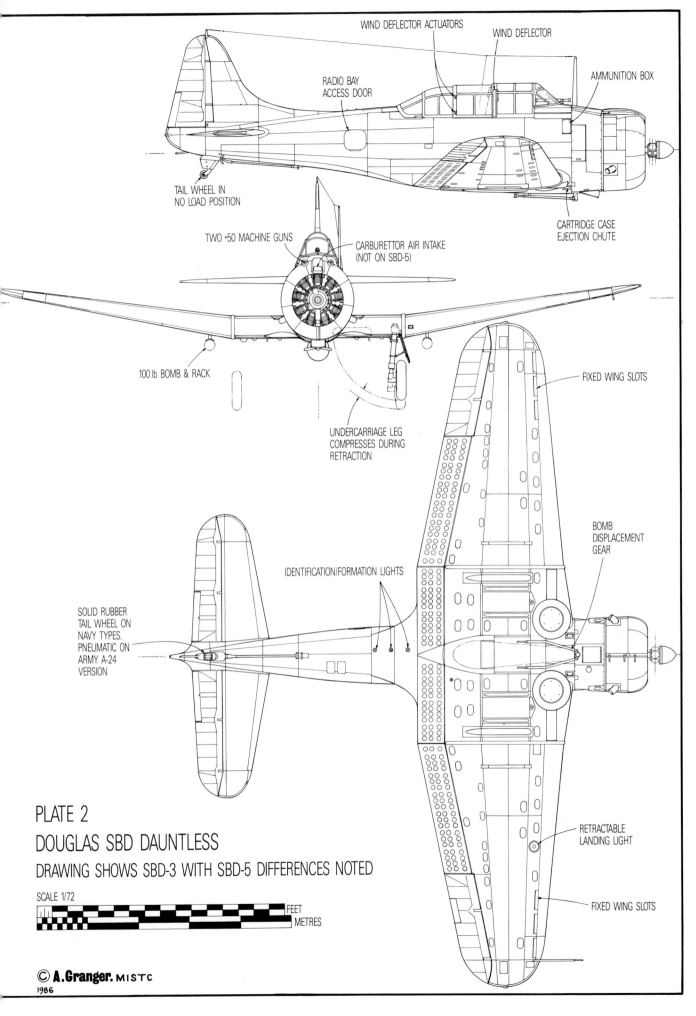

WIND DEFLECTOR ACTUATORS

WIND DEFLECTOR

AMMUNITION BOX

RADIO BAY
ACCESS DOOR

TAIL WHEEL IN
NO LOAD POSITION

CARTRIDGE CASE
EJECTION CHUTE

TWO ·50 MACHINE GUNS

CARBURETTOR AIR INTAKE
(NOT ON SBD-5)

100 lb BOMB & RACK

UNDERCARRIAGE LEG
COMPRESSES DURING
RETRACTION

FIXED WING SLOTS

IDENTIFICATION/FORMATION LIGHTS

BOMB
DISPLACEMENT
GEAR

SOLID RUBBER
TAIL WHEEL ON
NAVY TYPES.
PNEUMATIC ON
ARMY A-24
VERSION

RETRACTABLE
LANDING LIGHT

FIXED WING SLOTS

PLATE 2
DOUGLAS SBD DAUNTLESS
DRAWING SHOWS SBD-3 WITH SBD-5 DIFFERENCES NOTED

SCALE 1/72

FEET
METRES

© A. Granger. MISTC
1986

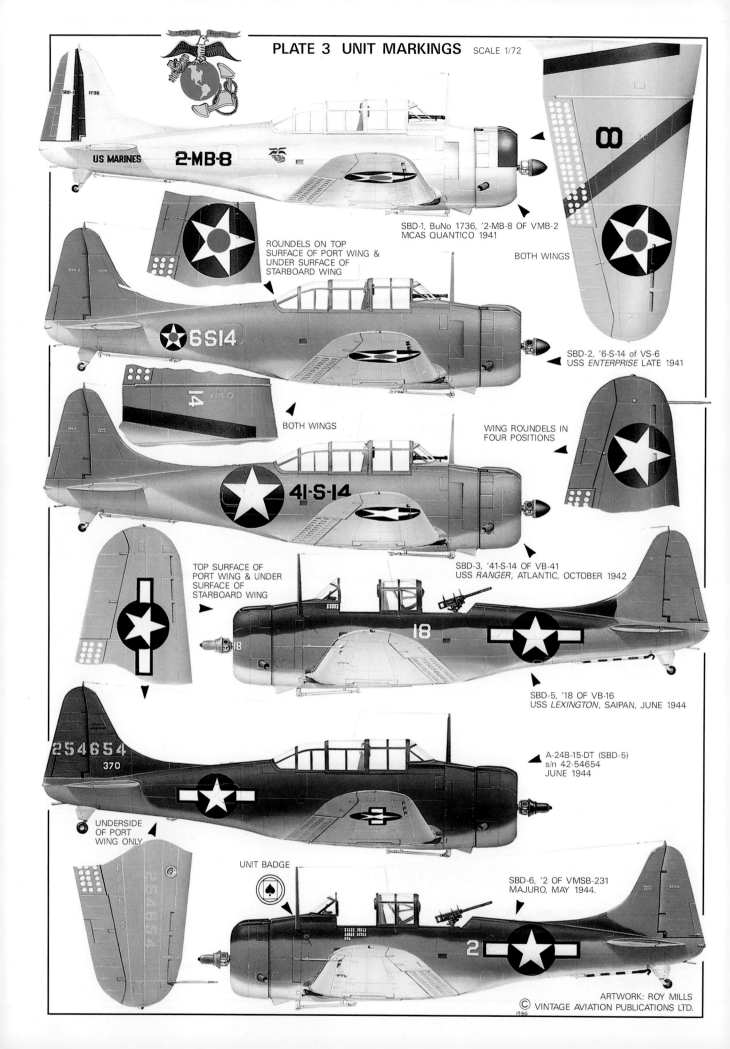

PLATE 3 UNIT MARKINGS SCALE 1/72

US MARINES 2-MB-8

SBD-1, BuNo 1736, '2-MB-8 OF VMB-2
MCAS QUANTICO 1941

BOTH WINGS

ROUNDELS ON TOP
SURFACE OF PORT WING &
UNDER SURFACE OF
STARBOARD WING

6 S14

SBD-2, '6-S-14 of VS-6
USS *ENTERPRISE* LATE 1941

BOTH WINGS

WING ROUNDELS IN
FOUR POSITIONS

41·S·14

TOP SURFACE OF
PORT WING & UNDER
SURFACE OF
STARBOARD WING

SBD-3, '41-S-14 OF VB-41
USS *RANGER*, ATLANTIC, OCTOBER 1942

18

SBD-5, '18 OF VB-16
USS *LEXINGTON*, SAIPAN, JUNE 1944

254654
370

A-24B-15-DT (SBD-5)
s/n 42-54654
JUNE 1944

UNDERSIDE
OF PORT
WING ONLY

UNIT BADGE

2

SBD-6, '2 OF VMSB-231
MAJURO, MAY 1944.

ARTWORK: ROY MILLS
© VINTAGE AVIATION PUBLICATIONS LTD.

Fig. 19 Part of a patrol flight in the South Pacific, 1942, including an SBD-3 and a quartet of TBFs. The markings are typical of the post-Midway period, with the large fuselage roundel without a red centre and the obviously overpainted tail. (NASM)

Fig. 20 An A-24B-DT, complete with stencilled Army serial on the tail. Colour is standard olive drab and neutral grey. Almost all A-24s carried the s/n repeated under the left wing. (NASM)

Fig. 21　The SBD-3 of Lt Turner F. Caldwell, CO of VS-5, launches off Enterprise *on D–Day of Operation Watchtower, the invasion of Guadalcanal, 7 August 1942. Bomb load was a single 500lb (227kg) bomb. Traditionally, scouting aircraft carried lighter bomb loads than their bombing counterparts, even if the VBs and VSs used the same aircraft. By the time the Fast Carrier Force was formed a year later, most VSs had been landed, their place on the carrier taken mainly by more fighters. (USN)*

As much of a success as the Dauntless proved to be with Navy or Marine pilots, it was consistently something less in any other hands. A case in point would be the experience of the USAAF. The Army Air Corps had toyed with the idea of ordering divebombers throughout the 1930s but finally did so only after observing the success of the German Stukas in Europe, 1939–40. Having delayed for so many years, they were now in a hurry, and, lacking time to develop their own designs, turned to the Navy for aircraft. In rapid succession, they ordered large quantities of Dauntlesses as A-24s and Helldivers as A-25s. Specifically, 168 SBD-3s were diverted from the Navy order and, with minimal modification (removal of tailhook and replacement of the solid tailwheel with a pneumatic one), were delivered with the dual designation, SBD-3A/A-24-DE. So similar was the A-24 to the SBD-3 that examples often alternated on the El Segundo production line. The USAAC tried to get a squadron of A-24s to the Philippines before war broke out, the 91st BS leaving California in November 1941, but it was too late. Diverted first to Brisbane and then to the Dutch East Indies, the 91st served with a singular lack of distinction. The same holds true for the 8th BG which came out to Australia

in 1942. Despite this lack of initial success in divebombing, the USAAF continued to acquire Dauntlesses; 170 SBD-4s became A-24A-DEs and 615 SBD-5s became A-24B-DTs. Some A-24Bs also saw combat, equipping the 531st FBS, which operated out of Makin Island in late 1943–4. This unit reported good results, but it faced no significant aerial opposition and the same success probably would have been achieved with virtually any aircraft.

The only visible difference between the SBD-3 and its successor, the SBD-4, was the replacement of its adjustable-pitch propeller with a Hamilton-Standard Hydromatic constant-speed model. The most significant change was internal, a switch over to a 24-volt power system to allow the installation of ASB radar. (Initial batch -4s did not have the radar fitted at the factory, some had it fitted in the field, most not at all. Only with later-production SBD-4s did the radar become a standard factory item.) The SBD-4 also introduced electric fuel pumps to the Dauntless for the first time. The production tempo continued to increase, 780 SBD-4s were built for the Navy. They went in large numbers to the Marines, where they were extensively employed in the continuing Solomons campaign.

Fig. 22 SBD-3s also saw action in the Atlantic. Here four Dauntlesses prepare for take-off from Santee, 25 September 1942. They were replaced on escort carriers as soon as Avengers became available. Santee retained its SBDs through the Torch landings in November, losing them shortly thereafter. (USN)

Fig. 23 An SBD-3 of Ranger's VS-41 catches a wire, 16 October 1942. Prior to Torch, the markings of Ranger's aircraft was standard except for the retention of full squadron coding. Because it was larger than the escorts, Ranger retained its Dauntlesses throughout its service in the Atlantic. (USN/NARS)

Fig. 24 Nearly identical A-24s and SBD-3s sit in the parking lot at El Segundo, 20 June 1941. The Army A-24s, in the foreground, are in olive drab and neutral grey. The SBDs, right-hand row, are in the outdated overall light grey scheme. The only visible differences are the absence of a tailhook on the A-24s (though the fairing for the hook remained) and the use of a pneumatic tailwheel. (Douglas)

Fig. 25   The SBD-4 visibly differed from the -3 only in the prop, which now had a prominent hub boss. Here, a -4 on Ranger *displays the temporary markings adopted for the Torch landings, a yellow surround to the fuselage roundel, November 1942. (USN/NARS)*

By the time the US Navy's carriers resumed the offensive in late 1943, its primary divebomber was the SBD-5, though the Dauntless's days were now numbered. (The first Helldiver squadron, *Bunker Hill*'s VB-17, arrived in November 1943.) The SBD-5 was the main production variant of the Dauntless, 2965 being built for the Navy along with the Army order and 60 more built for the Army which were retained by the Marines and designated SBD-5As. The -5 was powered by an uprated R-1820-62 of 1200hp. This was too small an increase over the earlier powerplant to make a great difference. Top speed rose only 7mph (11km/hr) to 252mph (406km/hr) and cruise speed actually fell due to

further weight increases. The most obvious external differences were an enlarged exhaust air slot behind the cowling and the deletion of the prominent air scoop above the cowling. This was the last "major" change in the SBD design. The follow-on SBD-6, of which only 451 were completed, was externally indistinguishable from the -5. It did feature a further increase in power with the installation of the 1350hp R-1820-66, which boosted top speed to 262mph (422km/hr), but by March 1944 this kind of performance was simply inadequate even for lesser campaigns and most -6s ended up as trainers or squadron hacks.

The Dauntless still had some battles to fight, though, before it was retired. Even as numbers dwindled in the fleet, they participated in raids on Marcus, Wake and the Palaus in fall 1943. At the time of the Gilberts campaign in November, five out of six VBs in TF50 still operated SBD-5s. The proportion was much the same at the time of the Truk raids in February 1944 (four out of five), but by June, and the Marianas campaign, only *Lexington*'s VB-16 and *Enterprise*'s VB-10 were completely equipped with Dauntlesses. (It was at this point in the SBD's career that its lack of wing-folding became most critical. It would have been natural for Dauntlesses, with their superb handling, to be assigned to CVL and CVE air groups, as was the Wildcat, but these smaller carriers were too cramped to take the SBD. Because of this and the fact that Helldrivers proved too dangerous on smaller flight decks, TBM Avengers became the standard attack aircraft in the escort and light carrier groups.)

The Battle of the Philippine Sea would be the last great carrier vs. carrier battle and the Dauntless's last fight as a first-line, carrier-based divebomber. That late afternoon, long-range strike at Ozawa's fleeing carriers was notable more for the skill of TF58's pilots in bringing back as many of their aircraft in the dark as they did, than for any offensive exploits. (The results of the air attacks were disappointing at best: one Japanese carrier sunk and two damaged.) 23 of 27 SBD-5s returned to their carriers, a far better percentage than any other type

involved (Hellcats lost over 25%, Avengers 65% and Helldivers 90% of those launched—in all, 104 of 216 aircraft never made it back to their carrier.)

Despite this good showing, the Dauntless's time had finally run out. The last carrier sortie was off *Enterprise* (fittingly enough) on 5 July 1944 against Guam. Marines continued to fly SBDs in the Solomons and Philippines until the end of the war. Even that does not totally end the tale. Despite the fact that Dauntlesses rapidly disappeared from all US service inventories after VJ-Day, other nations still found a use for the old bird. The French, whose Air Force and Navy both flew Dauntlesses in a ground support role over France after D-Day, used them again briefly over Indo-China postwar, but retired them in favour of Helldivers in 1949. The Mexicans probably flew the last Dauntless missions, using A-24Bs in an ASW role over the Caribbean until 1959.

No single quality of the Dauntless, not even its legendary handling, can account for the success that this aircraft achieved against all odds. That it was flown by excellent pilots is undeniable, though in the first months of the war, when it achieved its greatest success, the enemy was at least as good, maybe even better. That it was lucky (and lucky for those who flew it) is equally undeniable. Time and again it was at the right place at the right time. Most important, though, is the fact that, once there, it had the right combination of qualities and pilots to take full advantage of every break it got.

Fig. 26   When the Fast Carrier Force was formed in mid 1943, SBD-4s were the principal bombing type. 22-C-11 is prepared for take-off from In-dependence, 18 April 1943. Because of its lack of wing folding, the Dauntless didn't last long on light carriers. Only Independence *carried SBDs and these were replaced by TBMs after the first raids. (USN/NARS)*

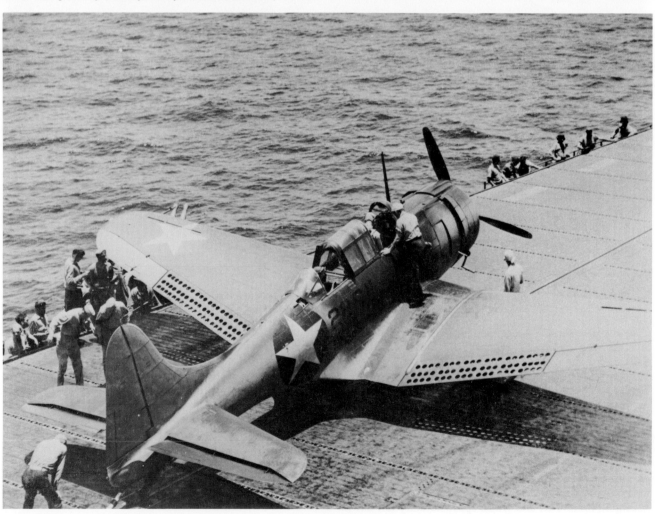

Fig. 27 **22-C-14, the 14th aircraft of VC-22 (Composite Squadron), has its twin-mount cleaned. This twin .30in (7.62mm) machine gun mounting became standard on the -4, having been introduced during the -3 run. In the place of the centreline tunnel, twin sliding panels were now provided to allow the guns to be lowered into the fuselage when not in use.** *(USN/NARS)*

Fig. 28 **SBD-5s carried the divebombing load in late 1943 and into 1944. Here, a pair of VB-5 Dauntlesses off** Yorktown **are seen during the Wake Island raids, 5–6 October 1943. Markings during this period were very plain. The three-colour camouflage was standard. The number of carriers had not yet built up to the point that there was confusion between air groups, hence the lack of distinctive markings.** *(NASM)*

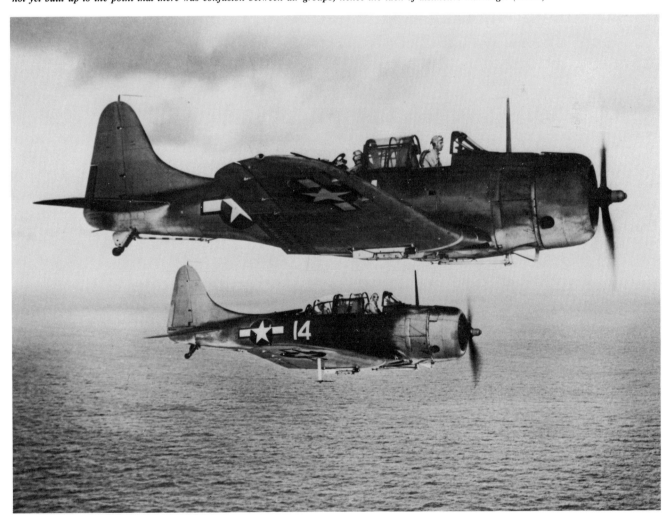

Figs. 29 & 30 Two views of VB-10 SBD-5s during the Palau raids, March 1944. These show to advantage the distinguishing marks of the type: the elongated exhaust slot behind the cowling, the lack of cowling air scoop and the now-standard Yagi antennas for the ASB radar. Enterprise's VB-10 would be the last unit to give up its Dauntlesses, in July 1944. (USN/NARS)

Fig. 31   Divebomber weather – Marine SBD-5s over New Britain, 28 March 1944. The scattered cumulus clouds hid divebombers until the last possible minute and offered sanctuary when attempting to elude pursuit. Directly below is the Warengoi River. In the background is Blanche Bay, leading directly to Rabaul, off the picture to the left. (USN/NARS)

Fig. 32 The Dauntless' last battle was the Philippine Sea. Virtually no photos exist of the most exciting part of that action, the dusk raid on Ozawa's fleet, because all of the camera planes were lost. This view of one of **Lexington's** *VB-16 SBD-5s was taken earlier in the day, 15 June 1944, over Saipan. Most of the fleet's attack aircraft spent the day circling Saipan, to keep the decks clear for fighters during the 'Turkey Shoot'. (USN/NARS)*

Fig. 33 While the Navy did not follow the Army's lead in reverting to natural metal for combattant aircraft, it did accept that finish for stateside-based trainers and utility aircraft. Since this was the role most late SBDs played, the number of shiny Dauntlesses rose sharply in 1945. Here, an SBD-5 is seen over a city in the western US. (NASM)

SPECIFICATIONS

XBT-2

Dimensions: length, 31ft 9in (9677mm); span, 41ft 6in (12649mm); height, 12ft 10in (3912mm); wing area, 320sq ft (29.7sq m).
Weights: loaded weight, 7593lb (3444kg); empty weight, 5093lb (2310kg).
Performance: max speed, 265mph (426km/hr); cruise speed, 155mph (249km/hr); rate of climb, 1450ft/min (442m/min); range (bombing), 604 miles (927km); range (scouting), 1485 miles (2390km).
Powerplant: Wright XR-1820-32 Cyclone of 1000hp takeoff power.
Armament: 2×.50 (12.7mm) machine guns fixed; 1×.30 (7.62mm) machine gun flexible; 2×100lb (45kg) bomb or depth charge; 1×500lb (227kg) or 1×1000lb (454kg) or 1×1600lb (726kg) bomb.

SBD-1

Dimensions: length, 32ft 2in (9804mm); span, 41ft 6in (12649mm); height, 13ft 7in (4140mm); wing area, 325sq ft (30.2sq m).
Weights: loaded weight, 9790lb (4441kg); empty weight, 5903lb (2678kg).
Performance: max speed, 253mph (407km/hr); cruise speed, 142mph (229km/hr); rate of climb, 1230ft min (375m/min); range (bombing), 860 miles; (1384km); range (scouting), 1165 miles (1875km).
Powerplant: Wright R-1820-32 Cyclone of 1000hp takeoff power.
Armament: 2×.50 (12.7mm) machine gun fixed; 1×.30 (7.62mm) machine gun flexible; 2×100lb (45kg) bomb or depth charge; 1×500lb (227kg) or 1×1000lb (454kg) or 1×1600lb (726kg) bomb.

SBD-2

Dimensions: length, 32ft 2in (9804mm); span, 41ft 6in (12649mm); height, 13ft 7in (4140mm); wing area, 325sq ft (30.2sq m).
Weights: loaded weight, 10,360lb (4699kg); empty weight, 6293lb (2855kg).
Performance: max speed, 252mph (406km/hr); cruise speed, 148mph (238km/hr); rate of climb, 1080ft min (329m/min); range (bombing), 1225 miles; (1971km); range (scouting), 1370 miles (2205km).
Powerplant: Wright R-1820-32 Cyclone of 1000hp takeoff power.
Armament: 1×.50 (12.7mm) machine gun fixed; 1×.30 (7.62mm) machine gun flexible; 2×100lb (45kg) bomb or depth charge; 1×500lb (227kg) or 1×1000lb (454kg) or 1×1600lb (726kg) bomb.

SBD-3

Dimensions: length, 32ft 8in (9957mm); span, 41ft 6in (12649mm); height, 13ft 7in (4140mm); wing area, 325sq ft (30.2sq m).
Weights: loaded weight, 10,400lb (4717kg); empty weight, 6345lb (2878kg).
Performance: max speed, 250mph (402km/hr); cruise speed, 152mph (245km/hr); rate of climb, 1190ft min (363m/min); range (bombing), 1345 miles; (2165km); range (scouting), 1580 miles (2543km).
Powerplant: Wright R-1820-52 Cyclone of 1000hp takeoff power.
Armament: 2×.50 (12.7mm) machine guns fixed; 1×.30 (7.62mm) machine gun flexible; 2×100lb (45kg) bomb or depth charge; 1×500lb (227kg) or 1×1000lb (454kg) or 1×1600lb (726kg) bomb.

SBD-4

Dimensions: length, 32ft 8in (9957mm); span, 41ft 6in (12649mm); height, 13ft 7in (4140mm); wing area, 325sq ft (30.2sq m).
Weights: loaded weight, 10,480lb (4753kg); empty weight, 6360lb (2885kg).
Performance: max speed, 245mph (394km/hr); cruise speed, 150mph (241km/hr); rate of climb, 1150ft min (351m/min); range (bombing), 1300 miles; (2092km); range (scouting), 1450 miles (2334km).
Powerplant: Wright R-1820-52 Cyclone of 1000hp takeoff power.
Armament: 2×.50 (12.7mm) machine guns fixed; 1×.30 (7.62mm) machine gun flexible; 2×100lb (45kg) bomb or depth charge; 1×500lb (227kg) or 1×1000lb (454kg) or 1×1600lb (726kg) bomb.

SBD-5

Dimensions: length, 33ft 0in (10058mm); span, 41ft 6in (12649mm); height, 13ft 7in (4140mm); wing area, 325sq ft (30.2sq m).
Weights: loaded weight, 10,700lb (4854kg); empty weight, 6533lb (2963kg).
Performance: max speed, 252mph (406km/hr); cruise speed, 152mph (245km/hr); rate of climb, 1700ft min (518m/min); range (bombing), 1115 miles; (1794km); range (scouting), 1565 miles (2519km).
Powerplant: Wright R-1820-60 Cyclone of 1200hp takeoff power.
Armament: 2×.50 (12.7mm) machine guns fixed; 1×.30 (7.62mm) machine gun flexible; 2×100lb (45kg) bomb or depth charge; 1×500lb (227kg) or 1×1000lb (454kg) or 1×1600lb (726kg) bomb.

CURTISS SB2C HELLDIVER

Fig. 1 *SB2C-3s of* **Lexington's** *VB-20 being catapult launched.* *(USN via Dick Hill)*

Fig. 2   In its original form, the XSB2C-1 as it appeared between December 1940 and August 1941. Except for the relatively small tail, all of the 'lines' of the Beast are there. The aircraft is overall aluminium with chrome yellow wings and stabilisers and black wingwalks. (Curtiss)

Few other aircraft in history have ever gained a less enviable reputation, yet served with as high a level of success as the SB2C Helldiver. Maybe it was because the Helldiver was the intended replacement for the Dauntless, one of the most popular aircraft ever to fly. Almost any aircraft would have fared poorly in comparison (and the Helldiver was not "any aircraft" when it came to handling). Maybe it was because it looked like it would never fly with that big tail. Indeed, that tail was its most distinguishing physical feature, leading to the Helldiver's most enduring nickname, "Big-Tailed Beast" or often just "Beast". Certainly it did have its share of development problems, particularly concerning handling, but so did many other aircraft which never earned the Helldiver's lasting notoriety. (Probably the most apt comparison is with the F4U Corsair, which, if anything, had even greater handling problems early in its career, but ended up being acknowledged as one of the most successful aircraft ever to fly.)

Perhaps none of these factors singly would have been sufficient to have ruined the Beast's reputation, but added together they made the Helldiver notorious long before it was issued to any combat units. So evil was the Helldiver's repute that a majority of front-line units resisted giving up their Dauntlesses as long as they could. Yet once they received their Beasts, they found it to be an effective bomber and a solid aircraft that brought home many a crew that should have ended up "in the drink". Even then the Beast was never loved but it did earn the begrudging respect of a lot of pilots in the brief time it was the US Navy's principal divebomber.

The ultimate irony is that the Helldiver eventually proved itself to be not only probably the best divebomber the Navy ever flew but also the last. Designed at a time when the divebomber, as a type, was on the ascendant, it entered service when the type was in decline. Combat experience had shown that even the best divebomber worked effectively in a relatively rare set of circumstances. In particular, it needed at least temporary air superiority. While the US enjoyed just such an advantage during most of the Helldiver's career, it obviously could not count on this always being the case. The Navy's attack aircraft in the postwar period would have to be even faster, more manoeuvrable and better able to defend themselves. In short, they would have to be more like a fighter-bomber, like the F4U which proved to be such a formidable attacker in the later stages of the war. Thus the Helldiver, which became the Navy's sole dedicated attack aircraft at war's end, displacing Avengers in the consolidated VAs (which replaced both VBs and VTs in 1947), was itself replaced by the Douglas AD Skyraider which was in every sense a new breed entirely.

The Helldiver had its origin in the Navy's awareness of the limitations of its new Dauntlesses. (The name Helldiver originated in the late 1920s when the F4C-4 was adopted as the Navy's standard divebomber. Since then any Curtiss-built Navy divebomber was known as Helldiver.) At the same time that the first SBDs were being ordered the search began for a successor, a divebomber that would be faster, have better range and carry a bigger load. Thus, in 1938, BuAer circulated a Request for Proposals (RFP) calling for all of this and more. The new scout-bomber was to be powered by the still experimental two-row, 14-cylinder Wright R-2600 Cyclone, was to carry a 1000lb (454kg) bomb in an internal bomb-bay (unlike the SBD which carried its payload externally) and two of the new bombers were to fit onto a 40ft × 48ft (12.2m × 14.6m) elevator with a foot (305mm) clearance all around. Six companies responded to the RFP, BuAer choosing Curtiss as the winner in May 1939, ordering a single prototype as the XSB2C-1. (As a back-up, BuAer also ordered a single XSB2A-1 from Brewster.)

From the beginning there was trouble. Wind tunnel testing on a small-scale wooden model of the XSB2C-1, begun in February 1940, indicated excessive stall speed and poor longitudinal stability. In an attempt to solve the first problem, the wing was increased in size from 385 to 422sq ft (35.8 to 39.2sq m). The other problem was less tractable, being the result of the very design parameters that controlled the Helldiver's shape. The critical requirement was for two of the new scout-bombers to fit on an elevator. This severely limited the length of the Helldiver while all of the other design requirements dictated an aircraft with considerably more internal volume than the SBD. The SB2C was to have 60% more power than the SBD-1, was twice as heavy yet was only four feet (1.2m) (18%) longer. When power, weight and size increase without a corresponding increase in length, the natural result is instability around the long axis. The only possible solution to the problem, as long as length cannot be significantly increased, is to increase the area of the vertical tail. This was done twice in the Helldiver's development without totally solving the problem. The Big-Tailed Beast's big tail was an inevitable result of the original BuAer RFP.

An additional complication, not that the XSB2C-1 needed more problems, was the Navy's insistence that the new Helldiver be mass-produced. Correctly perceiving that the World War would eventually embroil the US, BuAer early on informed Curtiss that it would be receiving orders of a magnitude not seen before by US aircraft manufacturers. 370 SB2C-1s were ordered while the prototype was still being assembled and within a year, before the first production example ever flew, that order was increased to 4000, of which 3000 were to be built by Curtiss. Thus, as the bugs were being worked out of the new aircraft, Curtiss would have to work through an even greater series of problems involving a new factory (at Columbus, OH), new mass-manufacturing techniques and a new work force, most of whom had never built an aircraft before.

The sole XSB2C-1 (BuNo 1748) was rolled out of Curtiss's Buffalo, NY, facility on 13 December 1940. Construction was conventional enough, with a semi-monocoque fuselage and a two-spar, four-section wing (two fixed centre sections and two folding outer sections), both aluminium-framed and alclad-skinned. (On the prototype, the wing centre section main frames were magnesium forgings.) All moving control surfaces were fabric-covered. Leading-edge slats were extended automatically when the landing gear was lowered to aid slow speed handling and lower the stall speed. Armament was a pair of .50cal (12.7mm) Browning machine guns in the cowling and one more in each wing, plus a

Fig. 3 After two months of revision, the prototype flew again in October 1941, flying in this condition until its loss in December. The tail has been enlarged and changed in shape in the first attempt to improve stability in the yaw axis. Toward the same end the nose has also been lengthened by a foot. (Curtiss)

twin .30cal (7.62mm) flexible mounting for the radio operator. In the original Helldiver mockup this mount was enclosed in a turret similar to that adopted for the TBF Avenger. In the prototype, however, it was replaced by a ring mount identical to the SBD's. In order to provide the gunner with the greatest possible field of fire, the entire upper rear fuselage "turtleback" folded down. The internal bomb-bay could accommodate a single 1000lb (454kg) bomb or two 500lb (227kg) bombs without modification, or a single 1600lb (726kg) bomb or Mk XVIII torpedo with simple adapter kits (with these weapons, the bomb-bay doors would not close completely). Power was provided by the 1700hp R-2600-8 Cyclone. This engine was officially beyond the experimental stage, but it was still very new and untried in production aircraft. It would eventually prove to be a powerful and reliable powerplant, but in December 1940 the Cyclone's teething problems only added to the Helldiver's.

With such an auspicious start, what followed surprised no-one. First flying on 18 December 1940, the XSB2C-1 crashed for the first time on 9 February when its Cyclone quit on final approach. Flying again on 6 May, it continued testing until August, missing another week in the process due to a collapsed landing gear leg. By August enough data had been gathered on the Beast's handling to set about solving the problems that had presented themselves. These included the predicted troubles with longitudinal stability and an unexpected problem

with tail buffetting in high speed dives. In an attempt at solving the yaw instability, the tail was enlarged for the first time and a foot (305mm) was added to the forward fuselage by extending the length of the engine mounts. The high speed instability was harder to tackle because in 1941 little was understood about the special problems associated with higher than normal speeds. No solution was attempted at this time beyond restricting the duration and angle of dives. (The high speed instability was eventually linked to its proper cause, compressibility effects created as an aircraft approaches the speed of sound. Perforated dive brake/flaps introduced in the late model SB2C-3 partially solved the problem, though the only complete cure was to restrict dive speeds.) At the same time an attempt was made to make the Cyclone more reliable by improving the cooling. The partial cowl flaps were extended completely around the cowling, cuffs were added to the propeller and a separate air scoop was provided for the oil cooler.

The XSB2C-1 flew again briefly in September 1941 in this form and then resumed flight tests in earnest on 20 October. Dive and spin tests continued until 21 December when the prototype was put into a "clean" dive from 22,000ft (6706m) with a maximum-g recovery at the bottom. The right wing and stabilizer gave way during pullout and the sole XSB2C-1 spun into the ground. For six months there was to be no flying Helldiver.

Fig. 4   The sheer size of the Beast presented a few problems for deckcrews, being by a good measure the biggest carrier-based aircraft to date. Power wing folding helped. Here an SB2C-1C of Essex's VB-15 is manhandled into position, 10 May 1944. Note the removable braces used to support the wings when the aircraft was parked. This is also a good view of the Yagi antenna. (NASM)

Fig. 5 SB2C-1Cs of VB-8 off **Bunker Hill** *prepare to launch during the Marianas campaign. By this time the number of carrier groups (CVGs) had risen to the point that some sort of distinctive marking was required.* **Bunker Hill** *was among the first, adopting the white line above and below the tail number as its insignia. (USN/NARS)*

Fig. 6 A pair of -1Cs of Yorktown's *VB-1 on patrol during the Marianas campaign. This view clearly shows the crooked pitot tube and twin .30in (7.62mm) gunner's mount which distinguish this mark from the previous.* Yorktown's *CVG-1 has adopted the slanting tail stripe as its distinction. (USN)*

Fig. 7 Because of the Beast's size and the marginal slow speed handling qualities of the early marks, barrier crashes were not infrequent. Here Hornet's deckcrew is seen in the process of disengaging a VB-2 SB2-1C from the wire, 19 July 1944. Fires in the space behind the engine were common in such situations and the crew is prepared. The lengthened engine mounts remained the weak point in the Helldiver's structure. They would frequently bend or fail altogether under abnormal stress. (USN/NARS)

Fig. 8 A pair of sinking ships mark the successful conclusion of a mission in the Philippines by this SB2C-3 of Hancock's VB-7, October 1944. The most noticeable distinctive feature of the -3 is the spinnerless four-bladed prop. Hancock's Omega sign can just be made out on the tail. (USN via Jim Sullivan)

Fig. 9 Four VB-19 SB2C-3s prepare to launch from **Lexington** *on 10 October 1944. The oversized tail number identified CVG-19. (USN/NARS)*

Fig. 10 Minus a chunk of its rudder, this SB2C-3 of **Intrepid's** *VB-18 taxies forward after landing, 25 October 1944. The white cross belonged to* **Intrepid's** *group. Note the folded-down turtleback. (USN via Dick Hill)*

Fig. 11 One VB-20 SB2C-3 launches off Lexington's port catapult while another is lined up on the starboard cat and a third waits its turn. Catapults came in very handy with big aircraft like the Helldiver, otherwise most of the deck was needed to get airborne. The tail triangle is white and the number black. (USN via Dick Hill)

Fig. 12 Escort carriers were found to be too small to successfully operate Helldivers but they were often used to ferry replacement Beasts for their bigger brothers. Here an SB2C rides out a typhoon lashed to the deck of Kwajelein (CVE-98), December 1944. (USN)

Fig. 13 As the number of air groups expanded rapidly over the course of 1944, the need for standardised markings led to 'geometric' series promulgated by COMAIRPAC on 27 January 1945. Here a VB-82 SB2C-3E, note the radar pod, rocket rails and perforated flaps, prepares to launch off Bennington, whose insignia under the new system was an arrowhead. Note the new overall glossy sea blue camouflage, February 1945. (USN via Dick Hill)

Fig. 14 *On 11 May 1945,* Bunker Hill *was hit by kamikazes, catching fire and burning fiercely for hours. One of VB-8's SB2C-4s was caught at the edge of the blaze. Note that the fabric cover of the ailerons is gone but that on the tail still remains. The large arrow was CVG-8's 'geometric' sign.* (USN/NARS)

Fig. 15 *A flight of CVG-9 Hellcats, Helldivers (SB2C-4s) and TBMs prepares to launch off* Yorktown *on 12 May 1945. Note the repetition of the white tail marking on the wingtip, part of the new marking regulations.* (USN via Dick Hill)

PLATE 1

CURTISS SB2C-5 HELLDIVER
'215 OF VB-9, USS *LEXINGTON*
JAPAN, SEPTEMBER 1945

SCALE 1/72

WHITE NUMBER ON
UNDERCARRIAGE DOOR
BOTH SIDES

WHITE AIRCRAFT NUMBER
ON LEADING EDGE OF
BOTH WINGS

UNDERSIDE OF
STARBOARD WING

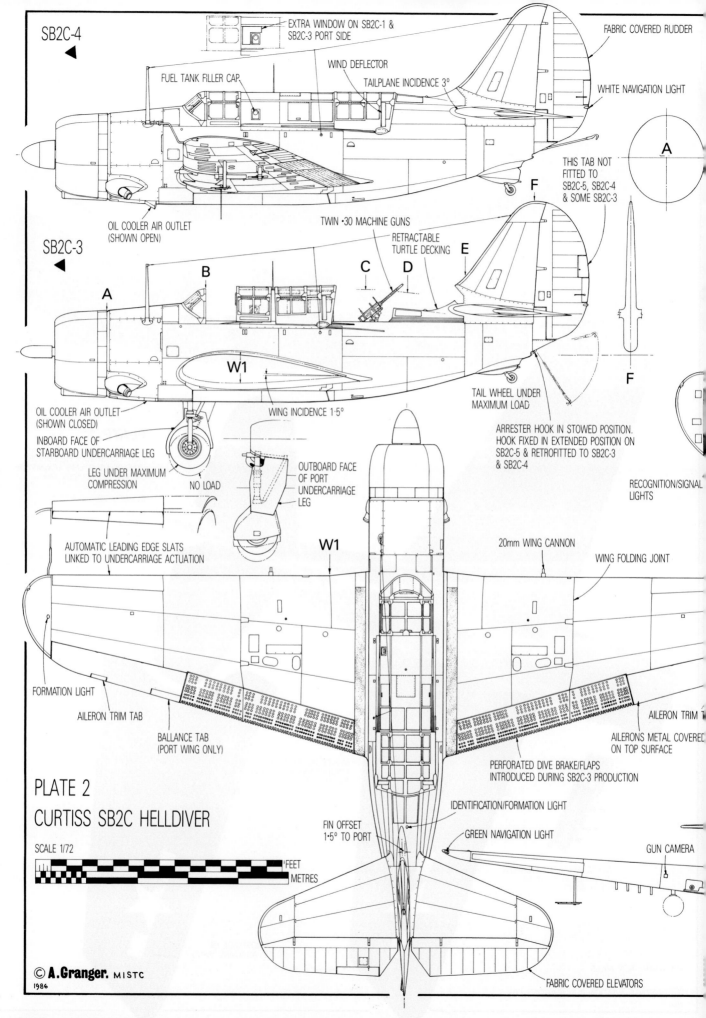

SB2C-4

EXTRA WINDOW ON SB2C-1 &
SB2C-3 PORT SIDE

FABRIC COVERED RUDDER

FUEL TANK FILLER CAP

WIND DEFLECTOR

TAILPLANE INCIDENCE 3°

WHITE NAVIGATION LIGHT

A

THIS TAB NOT
FITTED TO
SB2C-5, SB2C-4
& SOME SB2C-3

OIL COOLER AIR OUTLET
(SHOWN OPEN)

TWIN ·30 MACHINE GUNS

SB2C-3

RETRACTABLE
TURTLE DECKING

E

B

C

D

A

F

W1

WING INCIDENCE 1·5°

TAIL WHEEL UNDER
MAXIMUM LOAD

OIL COOLER AIR OUTLET
(SHOWN CLOSED)

INBOARD FACE OF
STARBOARD UNDERCARRIAGE LEG

ARRESTER HOOK IN STOWED POSITION.
HOOK FIXED IN EXTENDED POSITION ON
SB2C-5 & RETROFITTED TO SB2C-3
& SB2C-4

LEG UNDER MAXIMUM
COMPRESSION

NO LOAD

OUTBOARD FACE
OF PORT
UNDERCARRIAGE
LEG

RECOGNITION/SIGNAL
LIGHTS

AUTOMATIC LEADING EDGE SLATS
LINKED TO UNDERCARRIAGE ACTUATION

W1

20mm WING CANNON

WING FOLDING JOINT

FORMATION LIGHT

AILERON TRIM TAB

BALLANCE TAB
(PORT WING ONLY)

AILERON TRIM

AILERONS METAL COVERED
ON TOP SURFACE

PERFORATED DIVE BRAKE/FLAPS
INTRODUCED DURING SB2C-3 PRODUCTION

IDENTIFICATION/FORMATION LIGHT

PLATE 2
CURTISS SB2C HELLDIVER

FIN OFFSET
1·5° TO PORT

GREEN NAVIGATION LIGHT

GUN CAMERA

SCALE 1/72

FEET
METRES

© A. Granger. MISTC
1986

FABRIC COVERED ELEVATORS

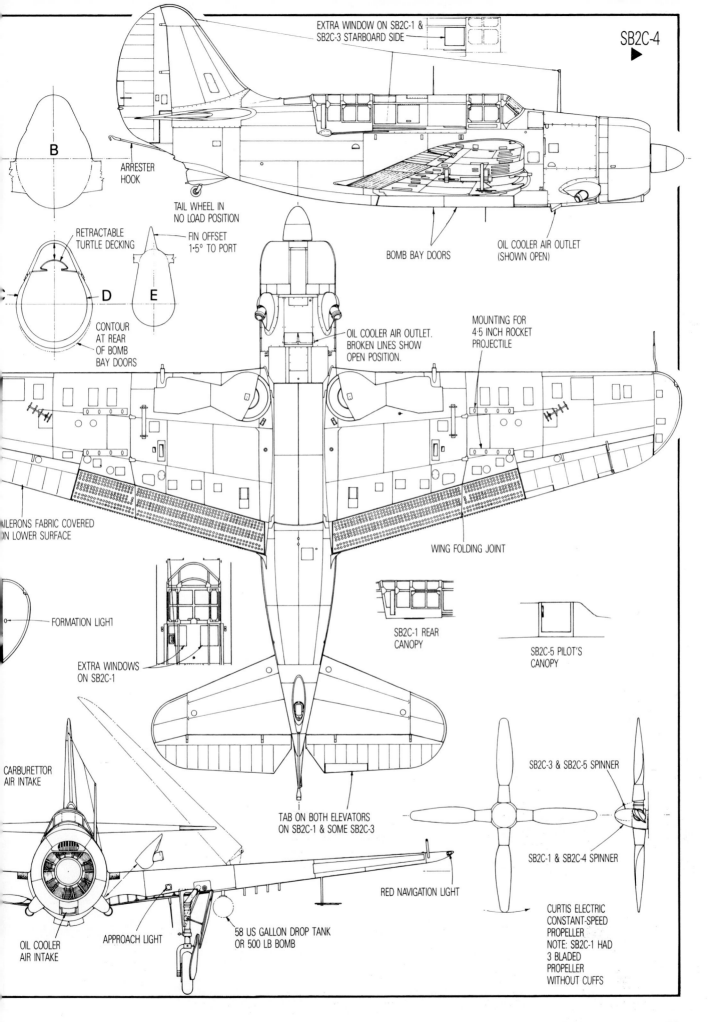

SB2C-4 ▶

EXTRA WINDOW ON SB2C-1 &
SB2C-3 STARBOARD SIDE

B

ARRESTER
HOOK

TAIL WHEEL IN
NO LOAD POSITION

RETRACTABLE
TURTLE DECKING

FIN OFFSET
1·5° TO PORT

D   E

CONTOUR
AT REAR
OF BOMB
BAY DOORS

BOMB BAY DOORS

OIL COOLER AIR OUTLET
(SHOWN OPEN)

OIL COOLER AIR OUTLET.
BROKEN LINES SHOW
OPEN POSITION.

MOUNTING FOR
4·5 INCH ROCKET
PROJECTILE

AILERONS FABRIC COVERED
ON LOWER SURFACE

WING FOLDING JOINT

FORMATION LIGHT

EXTRA WINDOWS
ON SB2C-1

SB2C-1 REAR
CANOPY

SB2C-5 PILOT'S
CANOPY

CARBURETTOR
AIR INTAKE

SB2C-3 & SB2C-5 SPINNER

SB2C-1 & SB2C-4 SPINNER

TAB ON BOTH ELEVATORS
ON SB2C-1 & SOME SB2C-3

RED NAVIGATION LIGHT

CURTIS ELECTRIC
CONSTANT-SPEED
PROPELLER
NOTE: SB2C-1 HAD
3 BLADED
PROPELLER
WITHOUT CUFFS

OIL COOLER
AIR INTAKE

APPROACH LIGHT

58 US GALLON DROP TANK
OR 500 LB BOMB

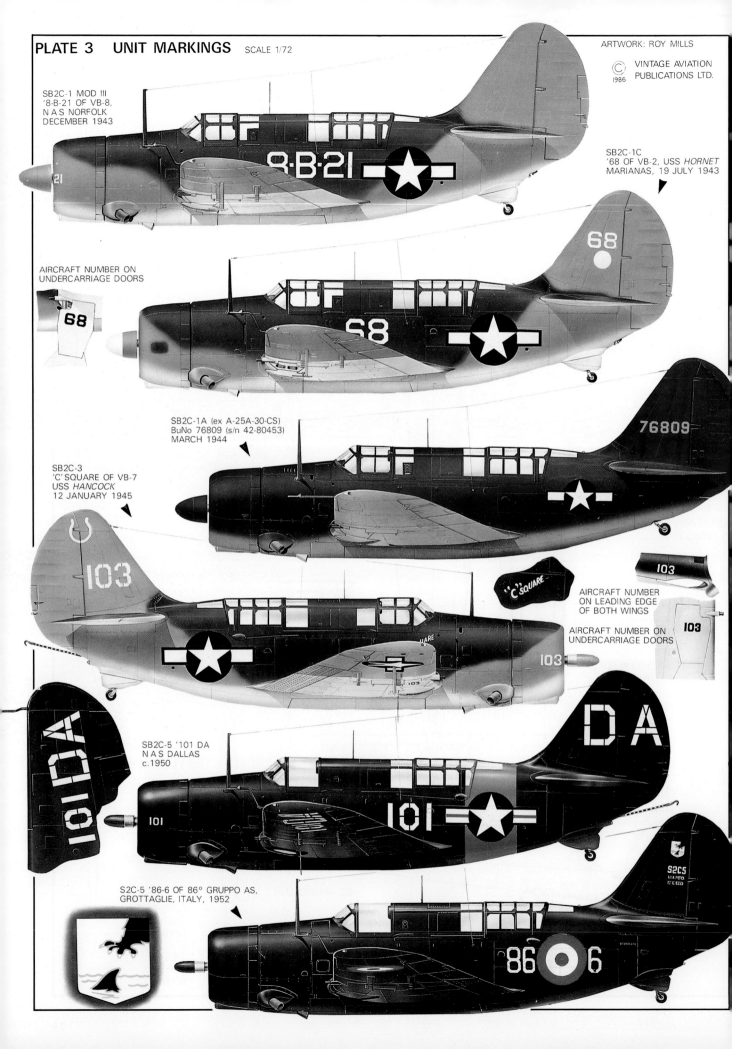

PLATE 3   UNIT MARKINGS   SCALE 1/72

ARTWORK: ROY MILLS

© 1986 VINTAGE AVIATION PUBLICATIONS LTD.

SB2C-1 MOD III
'8-B-21 OF VB-8,
N A S NORFOLK
DECEMBER 1943

SB2C-1C
'68 OF VB-2, USS HORNET
MARIANAS, 19 JULY 1943

AIRCRAFT NUMBER ON
UNDERCARRIAGE DOORS

SB2C-1A (ex A-25A-30-CS)
BuNo 76809 (s/n 42-80453)
MARCH 1944

SB2C-3
'C' SQUARE OF VB-7
USS HANCOCK
12 JANUARY 1945

"C" SQUARE

AIRCRAFT NUMBER
ON LEADING EDGE
OF BOTH WINGS

AIRCRAFT NUMBER ON
UNDERCARRIAGE DOORS

SB2C-5 '101 DA
N A S DALLAS
c.1950

S2C-5 '86-6 OF 86° GRUPPO AS,
GROTTAGLIE, ITALY, 1952

Fig. 16   5in (127mm) HVARs (High Velocity Artillery Rockets) are being loaded on the rocket rails of a VB-82 SB2C-4 on **Bennington,** *26 February 1945. Note the details of the perforated flaps introduced on the -3 and the air group markings repeated on the ailerons. (USN/NARS)*

BuNo 00001, the first produciton SB2C-1, had in fact been scheduled to fly in December 1941, but due to difficulties in starting up the assembly line was not ready until June 1942. When it finally did fly on 30 June, it differed externally from the prototype mainly in having a still larger tail. A number of other changes included reversion to a cuffless propeller, removal of the tail wheel doors, the repositioning of the cowl guns in the wings and the substitution of a single .50 (12.7mm) machine gun for the gunner's twin .30s (7.62mm). A reflector gunsight replaced the telescopic sight of the prototype and a DF loop was added to the cockpit and a bombrack and Yagi antenna for ASB radar under each wing. Less obvious changes included the addition of combat equipment such as an armoured glass windscreen, crew armour and self-sealing fuel tanks. Aluminium castings replaced the magnesium forgings in the wing centre sections. The result of these changes was a combat-ready aircraft with distinctly diminished performance, because empty weight rose by almost 3000lb (1361kg) to 10,114lb (4588kg). In the process top speed fell by 40mph (64km/hr) to 280mph (451km/hr) and landing speed rose by 10mph (16km/hr) to 79mph (127km/hr). While far from pleased with this deterioration in performance, BuAer had committed the Navy to the Helldiver programme and could only push ahead with production. (Later variants with more powerful versions of the Cyclone partially regained these losses.)

As rapidly as they could be produced, the first SB2C-1s were rushed into flight and service tests. These tests revealed myriad small (and not-so-small) problems, which generated so many individual ''fixes'', that it

soon became impossible to try to incorporate them into the assembly line and maintain anything resembling a production schedule. It became expedient to set up a separate modification line paralleling the assembly line at Columbus, taking completed SB2C-1s and modifying them to the current standard. The original modification set included mainly alterations to and restrictions on control surface movement. By April 1943, however, enough further changes had accumulated that a whole new standard (Mod II) was established, incorporating the previous changes (Mod I) and adding hundreds of further alterations. The most visible of these was the deletion of the DF loop and the adoption of a canted pitot tube. Mod III aircraft appeared in mid-'43, adding such changes as the reversion to twin .30s at the gunner's position and the locking down of the tail wheel. Only after 600 SB2C-1s (and -1Cs) were completed were all of the Mod III changes totally worked into the assembly line and the modification line shut down.

The first 200 Helldivers were completed as SB2C-1s, most of these leaving the Columbus plant as Mod IIIs. By early summer 1943 the number of new changes finally slowed to the point that BuAer felt it was practical to standardise on a definitive -1. The entire sequence of Mod III changes were included along with a number of other alterations. The two .50s in each wing were replaced by a single 20mm cannon and a slipstream baffle was added to the gunner's sliding canopy, deploying when the canopy was opened, to aid in the training of the flexible guns. 778 SB2C-1Cs were produced to this standard before being replaced on the production line by the SB2C-3 in spring 1944.

Fig. 17 One of the 10 A-25A-15-CSs eventually delivered to the RAAF, seen at St Louis on 9 August 1943. The camouflage is standard USAAF olive drab and medium grey, the markings are RAAF with blue and white roundels (with yellow surround on the fuselage) and an RAF-style fin flash. The A-25A 'froze' a number of SB2C-1 Mod I design features, in particular the straight pitot tube and the .50in (12.7mm) flexible machine gun. At this point the Shrike still retained the small retractable tail wheel used by the Navy. (Curtiss)

After a number of false starts, the Helldiver drew first blood on 11 November 1943. Originally intended for *Essex*'s air group and then *Yorktown*'s, both of those carriers having to leave for the front before the Beast was ready, the first batch of combat-worthy SB2C-1 Mod IIIs ended up in the capable hands of *Bunker Hill*'s VB-17. The results obtained by LCDR James E. "Moe" Vose's Helldivers over Rabaul on 11 November and later over Tarawa more than justified the labour required to get the Beast this far.

Still, it was spring 1944 before significant numbers of Helldiver-equipped (mainly SB2C-1Cs) VBs began to arrive with the fleet, in time for the last great carrier-vs-carrier engagement, the Battle of the Philippine Sea. While the immediate results of that engagement were ambiguous with regard to the Helldiver (only four Beasts were lost to enemy action but 39 out of the remaining 47 were forced to ditch or crashed on landing during the long return flight after dark), the long-term result was beneficial because the great losses of SB2C-1Cs led to the more rapid introduction of the considerably more powerful SB2C-3.

If the story of the Helldiver can be seen as the tale of an aircraft which matured at the same time as its "type" was becoming obsolete, then that of the A-25A Shrike was even more so. USAAC got into the divebomber business belatedly, getting seriously interested only after witnessing the great success of the Luftwaffe's Stukas in Poland and France. Obviously lacking the time to develop its own similar aircraft, the Army turned to existing Navy designs. SBD Dauntlesses were ordered in moderate quantities, with virtually no modification, as A-24s, while plans were laid to produce massive quantities of more modified SB2C-1s as A-25A Shrikes. (Shrike was another "traditional" name, all Curtiss-built Army attackers going back to the A-8 were named Shrike.) An order for 100 A-25As (Navy designation SB2C-1A) was placed on 31 December 1940, followed in spring 1942 by an order for 3000. With Curtiss's Columbus facility unable to meet Navy demands, it was obvious that the huge Army order would require a completely new assembly line. Therefore, at the end of

1941, USAAC's Materiel Command ordered Curtiss to switch its St Louis, MO, plant from the production of P-40s to A-25s.

Production Shrikes, which began to appear in late 1942, differed from their Navy counterpart in a number of features, mainly involving the removal of equipment required for carrier duty. All except the first Shrikes had their wing fold mechanism deleted and the wing slats locked closed (later still the slats were removed altogether). Similarly, radar and tailhook were deleted, while an inflatable tail wheel and larger main wheels were adopted during the production run. (In the interest of commonality and in an attempt to simplify subcontractor orders, the Navy adopted a few of the Army modifications for its Helldivers, most noticeably the larger main wheel and its associated larger wheelwell.)

In all 900 A-25A Shrikes were built between late 1942 and early 1944. Unfortunately, they no longer were required. Further combat in Europe, most notably the Battle of Britain, had shown up the divebomber's weakness in situations where air superiority did not exist. Even more importantly, the range and payload demands made by USAAF of its tactical bombers in Europe prior to D-Day strongly favoured twin-engine medium bombers over any divebomber. Even after the invasion, close air support could be provided by the existing medium bombers and by rocket-armed heavy fighters like the Thunderbolt and Typhoon. (Like the Navy and the Corsair, many USAAF commanders preferred arming a fighter with rockets or bombs to employing a purpose-built tactical bomber. After the rockets were fired and the bombs dropped, a Corsair or Thunderbolt remained a fully capable fighter, while a bomber was just a target.) Even the Australians, who had contracted for 150 Shrikes, changed their mind and refused shipment. Eventually the Navy took back 410 Shrikes as SB2C-1As for the Marines, the Army retaining the rest for training and target tug duties. Although most of the missing Navy equipment was reinstated on the Marine Shrikes, they saw no more combat than their Army counterparts, being considered decidedly inferior to the new SB2C-3s and -4s then coming off the line.

Fig. 18 An anomaly in flight, one of the SB2C-1As built for the Army at St Louis but turned over to the Marines when the Army decided it did not need its Shrikes after all. A very late production example, actually an A-25A-30-CS (s/n 42-80453) built in late 1943, this aircraft still displays the large pneumatic tail wheel characteristic of later Shrikes. Of greatest interest is the fact that despite being painted in perfect Army-style olive drab/medium green and neutral grey, the number displayed on its tail in Army-style insignia yellow numbers is its Navy BuNo, 24 March 1944. (Curtiss via Jim Sullivan)

Fig. 19 The sole XSB2C-2 is seen on a take-off run at NAS Norfolk. The added ventral fin can just be seen in the spray. (Art Whittaker via Jim Sullivan)

One other Helldiver offshoot was developed. As with the Wildcat and Devastator, BuAer attempted to create a float-Helldiver for use in the South Pacific. (The interest in float-based tactical aircraft stemmed from the use of the same by the Japanese and the perceived need for aircraft which could operate away from carriers or airfields.) Known as the XSB2C-2, a single SB2C-1 (BuNo 00005) was modified by the replacement of its normal landing gear by a pair of large Edo floats and the addition of a ventral fin. Except for an excessively long take-off run, the XSB2C-2 proved to be a satisfactory float-bomber and an order for 294, to be modified from normal Helldivers coming off the Columbus line, was placed in mid-1943. By the time enough Helldivers were available for conversion to begin, the need for such float-equipped combat aircraft had disappeared. (Escort carriers filled the void, providing local airpower wherever needed until airfields could be constructed.) The SB2C-2 order was cancelled in April 1944.

"Mainstream" Helldiver development continued with the SB2C-3. The most significant change was the adoption of a more powerful version of the Cyclone, the 1900hp R-2600-20. At the same time, a four-bladed spinnerless propeller was added to take better advantage of the increased power. Top speed increased somewhat, from 281mph (452km/hr) to 294mph (473km/hr), and the improvement in handling throughout the envelope was significant. Other changes included a revised rear canopy. Further significant alterations were adopted during the model run. After mid-production, approximately 10% were completed to SB2C-3E standard, the

difference being in electronics. "E" variants carried AN/APS-4 airborne intercept radar in a pod in the place of the ASB surface-search set. The characteristic Yagi antennae were removed and were replaced by the APS-4 pod carried under the starboard wing. (Since the radar pod was removable and often was removed if not needed for a particular mission, the surest identifier of an "E" variant is the lack of Yagi antennae.) SB2C-3Es were often employed in a similar fashion as radar-equipped Avengers, as formation aircraft for night fighter squadrons which would home in on targets based on contacts gained by the Helldiver. Late in the production run, perforated dive brakes were adopted, which not only helped solve the tail buffeting at high speed but also significantly improved the Beast's slow speed characteristics. Production was now in high gear, involving not only Curtiss but two Canadian firms as well. 1112 SB2C-3s were built at Columbus and a further 413 were completed as SBW-3s by Canadian Car & Foundry Ltd and 150 SBF-3s by Fairchild-Canada Ltd.

The most produced of the Helldiver variants was the SB2C-4, though it differed little from a late -3. The only visible changes included the addition of a spinner to the prop, the deletion of some of the small windows in the fixed canopy and the fitting of four zero-length rocket launchers under each wing outer panel. As with the -3, a percentage of SB2C-4s were delivered as -4Es, with the same alterations. 2045 SB2C-4s were built by Curtiss, 270 SBW-4Es by CC&F and 100 SBF-4Es by Fairchild. The SB2C-4 was the last Helldiver variant to see significant combat, arriving with the fleet in time to participate in the "Empire" raids of 1945.

Fig. 20 The 'geometric' markings proved to be difficult to describe over radio, so they were replaced by the 'G' symbol system of one or two letter codes on 27 July 1945. Lexington's letter was 'H'. This VB-9 SB2C-4 apparently hit the aft 5in (127mm) mount on landing, losing its engine in the process, 14 August 1945. (USN/NARS)

Fig. 21   This SB2C-5 caught the first barrier and is busy trying to dig a hole in the deck as it is coming to rest, 25 September 1945. Note the frameless pilot's canopy and the paddle-bladed prop. Note also the retention of **Lexington's** *'geometric' stripe long after the promulgation of the 'G' symbols and, indeed, after the end of the war. (USN/NARS)*

While a significant number, over 3000, SB2C-5s were ordered, the end of the war limited actual deliveries to a relatively small number. Differences from the preceding mark again were minor. A frameless pilot's canopy is probably the -5's most distinguishing feature. The tailhook was fixed in an extended position and Yagi antennae were no longer fitted because the ASB radar was deleted. (Essentially, the ''E'' variant had now become the standard.) Internally 35 more gallons (132lt) of fuel were carried to improve range. 470 were built at Columbus and 85 were delivered as SBW-5s by CC&F.

The SB2C-5 arrived too late to see significant action in WW2, but it became the standard US Navy attack aircraft in the postwar fleet, not being finally phased out by Skyraiders until June 1949. In other countries, the -5 saw even longer service, being used in combat by at least three air forces. Under MDAP, Helldivers went to Greece, Italy, France, Portugal and Thailand. The Greeks flew approximately 20 SB2C-5s in combat during the communist insurgency of the late '40s. Similarly the French and Thais used Helldivers in Indo-China against the Viet Minh. Of the five nations, the French were the only ones to operate their Beasts from carrier decks. Esc. 3.F earned fame flying close support

missions from *Arromanches* during the Dien Bien Phu campaign in 1954. The last nation to give up its Helldivers was Italy, which flew its S2C-5s (not being allowed bombers by treaty, the Italians dropped the ''B'' from the Beast's designation) until February 1959.

An SB2C-6 was planned, to be powered by the 2100hp R-2600-22. Two prototypes were built and the type did show considerable promise with improvement in all performance categories. The war was almost over by the time the XSB2C-6s flew, however, and BuAer saw no need for more divebombers. No production examples were ever built.

The Helldiver's story is curious from beginning to end. Like other aircraft that gained bad reputations, such as the Douglas Devastator, it was seemingly the wrong aircraft at the wrong time. But unlike the Devastator, the Helldiver saw great success in its long and active career. Like the Vought Corsair it suffered serious handling deficiencies early in its life and, like the Corsair, it took an inordinately long time to reach its intended squadrons. The main difference is that while the Corsair represented a type still on the ascendant (to this day), the big, powerful fighter/bomber, the Helldiver was the last of a dying breed, the last divebomber.

Fig. 22 Seen on 27 August 1944, one of the two XSB2C-6s shows the extended and rounded cowling adopted to enclose the more powerful R-2800-28. Two carburettor inlets at the upper corners of the cowling replaced the single inlet of earlier Beasts. (USN/NARS)

Fig. 23 After the war, -4 Helldivers were parcelled out to reserve units. All the markings, except for the national insignia, are orange. Until 1947, reserve aircraft had no fuselage roundel. To indicate its 'retired' status, this aircraft has been redesignated an N-SB2C-4E. (NASM)

Fig. 24 The immediate post-war period was one of great confusion in unit structure and markings, not brought under control until the general reorganisation of 1947. Some units, like VB-153, took up pre-war style unit and mission designator markings. (Art Whittaker via Jim Sullivan)

Fig. 25 During this period, tail markings could mean almost anything. Shore-based units, reserve or regular Navy, often used single letter codes that repeated the CVG letter assignments that were then, technically, in effect. The lack of lower landing gear door on this SB2C-5 seems to be the most important clue here. These were regularly removed on land-based aircraft to prevent mud build-up (not a problem on carrier decks). The 'C' then probably stands for NAS Columbus. The unit is probably regular Navy, given the lack of orange band, August 1945. (Warren A. Bodie via NASM)

Fig. 26 Unit identification becomes easier after 1947 as the new rules came into effect. The 'PS' code here identified aircraft of CVG-9 based on Philippine Sea. This is a flight of VA-9A SB2C-5s seen on 1 April 1948. (USN)

Fig. 27 Even in July 1948, things can get confusing. Here the second aircraft of VB-82, as can be ascertained from the full designator markings under the wing, carries only the aircraft number on fuselage and tail., Pittsburgh, PA. (USN via Jim Sullivan)

Fig. 28 Aeronavale Esc. 3.F flew SB2C-5s in relief of the garrison at Dien Bien Phu off **Arromanches,** *the Beast's last carrier-based combat operations. (Aeronavale)*

SPECIFICATIONS

SB2C-1C

Dimensions: length, 36ft 9in (11201mm); span, 49ft 9in (15164mm); height, 14ft 9in (4496mm), wing area, 422sq ft (39.2sq m)
Weights: gross weight, 13,674lb (6203kg), empty weight, 10,114lb (4588kg).
Performance: max speed at 12,400ft (3780m), 281mph (452km/hr); rate of climb, 1750ft min (533m/min); range, 1110 miles (1786km); ceiling, 24,200ft (7376m).
Powerplant: Wright R-2600-8 Cyclone of 1700hp takeoff power.
Armament: 2×20mm cannon, 2×.30 (7.62mm) machine guns flexible, 2×100lb (45kg) bomb or depth charge, 2×500lb (227kg) or 1×1000lb (454kg) or 1×1600lb (726kg) bomb or 1×Mk XVIII torpedo.

SB2C-4

Dimensions: length, 36ft 9in (11201mm); span, 49ft 9in (15164mm); height, 14ft 9in (4496mm), wing area, 422sq ft (39.2sq m)
Weights: gross weight, 14,189lb (6436kg), empty weight, 10,547lb (4784kg).
Performance: max speed at 16,700ft (5090m), 295mph (474km/hr); rate of climb, 1800ft min (549m/min); range, 1165 miles (1875km); ceiling, 29,100ft (8870m).
Powerplant: Wright R-2600-20 Cyclone of 1900hp takeoff power.
Armament: 2×20mm cannon, 2×.30 (7.62mm) machine guns flexible, 2×100lb (45kg) bomb or depth charge, 2×500lb (227kg) or 1×1000lb (454kg) or 1×1600lb (726kg) bomb or 1×Mk XVIII torpedo.

GRUMMAN TBF/TBM AVENGER

Fig. 1   A yellow cowl ring was adopted as a temporary marking by several air groups during February 1945. This TBM-3 of Bunker Hill's *VT-8 is seen on 17 February en route to Yokohama. (USN/NARS)*

Fig. 2 The XTBF-1 mock-up, seen at Bethpage in 1941. Not visible in this view is the lack of characteristic tail fillet which marked the first prototype. Except for that and the split wheel covers, which were deleted, this mock-up looks surprisingly similar to the production Avenger. (Grumman)

Rarely in the history of aviation has an aircraft been as consistently successful from its first flight or passed through its production life with as little alteration to its basic shape as the Grumman Avenger. Other aircraft have been more graceful, have flown faster or earned more glory, but none seemed to perform every task to which it was assigned with such ease. A sound basic design with plenty of extra interior space enabled the TBF/TBM to extend its career far beyond its normal span by demonstrating early in its life an adaptability rivaled by few other aircraft. Long after nearly all of its contemporaries were consigned to the smelter, Avengers were soldiering on in the colours of many nations (and even in civilian service) performing an incredible variety of jobs.

Still, what is most remarkable about the Grumman Avenger was its almost total lack of handling deficiencies throughout its career. From its first flight, it displayed pleasant flight characteristics at all speeds and altitudes. The only warning listed in the pilot's manual was a stern caution against deliberate spins. Once an Avenger started spinning, it was virtually impossible to recover. A crash was inevitable and a fast exit was advised. As a bombing platform, the TBF/TBM was stable in level flight and in shallow dives and retained that stability when flying low and slow in a torpedo run or on approach to a carrier landing. It could even make a passable divebomber with landing gear extended as dive brakes. The overriding impression one is left with is that of an aircraft with pleasant, unexceptional handling and average speed and range. While few ever labelled the Avenger an outstanding aircraft, no one ever called it inadequate.

The TBF/TBM started out as a general BuAer Request for Proposals issued in 1939. It specified a new torpedo bomber/level bomber to replace the TBD Devastator which had been in service since 1937, but was already being made obsolete by the tremendous pace of aircraft development. While not specifying the exact desired configuration of its new torpedo bomber, BuAer was sufficiently explicit that most of the submissions were for very similar aircraft. All called for a crew of three (pilot, bombardier and radio operator) each of which

were armed with a defensive weapon. In most proposals this was a single fixed .50 (12.7mm) machine gun for the pilot, a turretted, aft-firing .50 for the radio operator and a flexible, aft-firing .30 (7.62mm) for the bombardier to protect the tail from below. The choice of powerplant was left up to the individual company. The only requirement was that there be a significant increase in top speed over the TBD's 206mph (332km/hr). Offensive weaponry (a single Mk XIII torpedo or any combination of bombs, mines or depth charges up to 2000lb (907kg) was to be carried internally. Two firms won contracts for a pair of prototypes each, Grumman receiving the orders to build two XTBF-1s on 8 April 1940. Chance Vought was ordered to build two very similar XTBU-1s on 23 April.

The development of the XTBF-1 was so uneventful as to be almost boring. Only the requirement that the radio operator's weapon be enclosed in a powered turret caused any headaches. Power turrets as such were not new but their application to single-engine aircraft (in particular the RAF's experience with its turret fighters, the Blackburn Roc and Boulton-Paul Defiant) had been something less than salutary. These failures can be traced, among other causes, to the excess weight and slow traverse of earlier mechanical or hydraulic turrets. To solve both of these problems, Grumman engineer Oscar Olsen was assigned the task of designing an electrically driven turret. The problem with electrical turrets was that the loads on various points in the circumference of the turret would differ at different flight attitudes. Normal electric motors that would perform well when the aircraft was flying straight and level would fail when the aircraft went into a violent manoeuvre, which is often exactly when it was needed most. The answer was found in a new type of motor, the amplidyne motor, which could be varied rapidly in torque and speed and could be synchronised with other motors. These motors were already known in large-scale industrial applications. No one before Olsen, however, had considered using small amplidyne motors. At his request General Electric built two experimental models by hand, which were tested on the turret of the first XTBF-1. So succesful did they prove (again boring) that both motors and turret went into mass-production without modification.

Fig. 3   An early production TBF-1, seen in 1942. The only area of the Avenger that would see significant alteration during its production life was the cowling.   (Grumman)

Fig. 4 En route to disaster, 8-T-1 is seen on 26 March 1942, probably at NAS North Island. All of the red markings and the tail stripes would disappear, otherwise this was the condition in which it flew at Midway. (USN)

Fig. 5 After the battle, 8-T-1 is seen on Sand Island, Midway, 4 June 1942, the only survivor of the VT-8 aircraft engaged that day. (USN/NHC)

Fig. 6 An early Marine TBF-1 is photographed in 1942. The black marking on its tail is a landing assistance stripe, rarely painted that colour. Marines first took Avengers into combat in November 1942. (USN)

The XTBF-1 which flew for the first time on 7 August 1941 was primarily the handiwork of Grumman's Assistant Chief Engineer Bob Hall. While incorporating the new electrical turret and such new (for Grumman) features as wing-mounted, inward-retracting landing gear and fixed, ''letter-box'' leading edge slots, the Avenger prototype looked very much like a scaled-up Wildcat and did incorporate many of that earlier aircraft's external features. Both aircraft had a deep fuselage with a big radial engine in a tapering cowling and a mid-mounted, square-tipped, equal-taper wing with similar tail surfaces. From a distance and from most angles, the two aircraft were indistinguishable. (This similarity, particularly from below, caused many a mistaken identity. Perhaps the most famous case was that of the leading surviving Japanese naval ace Saburo Sakai who came up below a flight of three Avengers near Guadacanal, thinking they were Wildcats. The three bombardiers withheld fire until Sakai was at point-blank range and then saturated his Zero with .30 cal fire. Wounded in several places, his windscreen shattered and his aircraft barely functioning, Sakai incredibly piloted his aircraft all the way back to Rabaul, despite passing out from loss of blood on several occasions.)

The Avenger's construction was unexceptional. The oval-section fuselage was semi-monocoque and, along with the single-spar, power-folded wing, was all metal. All moving surfaces were metal framed and fabric covered. Power was provided by the still-new Wright R-2600-8 Cyclone 14, 14-cylinder, two-row radial of 1700hp takeoff power. This, driving a three-bladed Hamilton-Standard variable-pitch propeller, powered the prototype to a top speed of 271mph (436km/hr), the

desired significant advance over the TBD.

Testing of the first XTBF-1 (BuNo 2539) proceeded almost without event until 28 November 1941 when it was totally destroyed as the result of an in-flight electrical fire in the bomb bay. The only complaint against the Avenger to that point concerned a slight tendency to lateral instability which was cured on the second prototype (and on all succeeding examples) by the addition of a fillet between the fuselage and the vertical tail. This second XTBF-1 (BuNo 2540) flew on 20 December 1941. The nearness of this date to the Pearl Harbor attack led Grumman, with BuAer's blessing, to give their new bomber the name Avenger. Three days later, Grumman received an order for 286 TBF-1s, the first being delivered only 11 days later. (It is interesting to compare the development records of the TBF and SB2C, as they represent two opposite extremes. The Helldiver prototype was ordered 11 months before the first Avenger and flew eight months earlier but didn't enter combat until 17 months after the TBF. Some account must be taken of the difference in the need for the two aircraft, though of course the main cause of the differing time spans was the difference in the flying qualities of the aircraft themselves. Still, it should not be forgotten that TBFs were needed desperately to replace the woefully inadequate TBD which existed in the fleet in small and rapidly dwindling numbers. When they were gone, there would be no torpedo bombers for the fleet until the first Avengers arrived. The Helldiver, on the other hand, was the intended replacement for the obsolescent, but very popular and still quite capable and plentiful, SBD and BuAer certainly never felt the same urgency to get SB2Cs to the front.)

Fig. 7 A TBF-1, 26-GS-10, is hauled on board Charger, 13 July 1942, for training. Air groups intended for US escort carriers were originally designated VGS (G for escort, S for scout), later redesignated VC (C for composite). VGS-26 was to be Sangamon's (CVE-26) air group. (USN/NARS)

Figs. 8 & 9 FN755 was the sixth Royal Navy Tarpon I (Avenger I, TBF-1, BuNo 0629). It has apparently suffered structural damage on landing on Charger, 1 November 1942. Charger was manned by the US Navy but was used almost exclusively for the training of RN crews. (USN/NARS)

97

Fig. 10 The only Avenger to serve on Ranger during the Torch landings in November 1942 was this TBF-1, the personal mount of CAG-9, Cdr D. B. Overfield, 26 August 1942. (USN/NARS)

Fig. 11   22-C-2, a TBF-1 of VC-22 off Independence is seen launching on 1 May 1943. The noticable gun trough for the single forward-firing .50in (12.7mm) instantly identifies a -1. (USN/NARS)

Figs. 12 & 13   56 of VT-16 appears to have caught fire while being positioned on Lexington's deck-edge elevator. Fire extinguishers are being passed up the wing to crewmen fighting the fire from above while a panel has been removed and CO_2 is being applied from below, to the uncertain reaction of some obvious sceptics, 4 June 1943. (USN/NARS)

Fig. 14 The art of loading a torpedo rapidly had to be practised repeatedly during training, so that it could be done efficiently in battle. Most of the actual work done by the hand winch, seen just outside the bomb bay to the left, which was inserted through a hole in the fuselage. SB2Cs employed a similar but different winch, hence the markings on this one, Lexington, 12 September 1943. (USN/NARS)

ARTWORK: ROY MILLS

© VINTAGE AVIATION PUBLICATIONS LTD.
1986

PLATE 1

GRUMMAN TBM-3E AVENGER
BuNo 53688, 401SK
10 MARCH 1950

SCALE 1/72

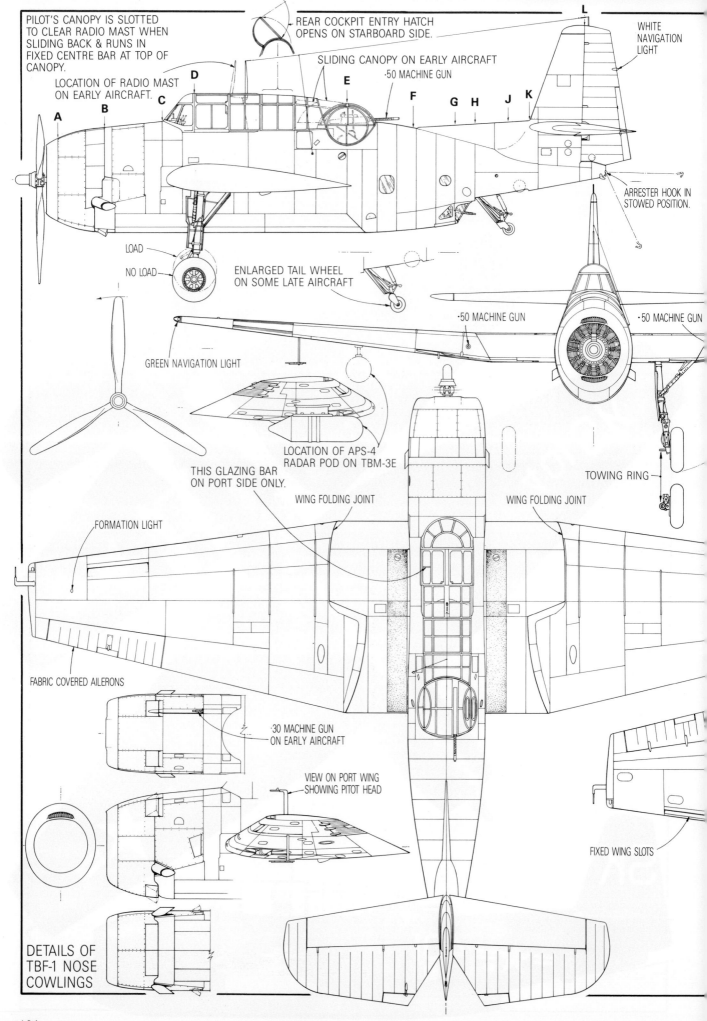

PILOT'S CANOPY IS SLOTTED TO CLEAR RADIO MAST WHEN SLIDING BACK & RUNS IN FIXED CENTRE BAR AT TOP OF CANOPY.

REAR COCKPIT ENTRY HATCH OPENS ON STARBOARD SIDE.

SLIDING CANOPY ON EARLY AIRCRAFT
·50 MACHINE GUN

WHITE NAVIGATION LIGHT

LOCATION OF RADIO MAST ON EARLY AIRCRAFT.

A   B   C   D   E   F   G H   J   K   L

ARRESTER HOOK IN STOWED POSITION.

LOAD
NO LOAD

ENLARGED TAIL WHEEL ON SOME LATE AIRCRAFT

·50 MACHINE GUN   ·50 MACHINE GUN

GREEN NAVIGATION LIGHT

LOCATION OF APS-4 RADAR POD ON TBM-3E

TOWING RING

THIS GLAZING BAR ON PORT SIDE ONLY.

WING FOLDING JOINT   WING FOLDING JOINT

FORMATION LIGHT

FABRIC COVERED AILERONS

·30 MACHINE GUN ON EARLY AIRCRAFT

VIEW ON PORT WING SHOWING PITOT HEAD

FIXED WING SLOTS

DETAILS OF TBF-1 NOSE COWLINGS

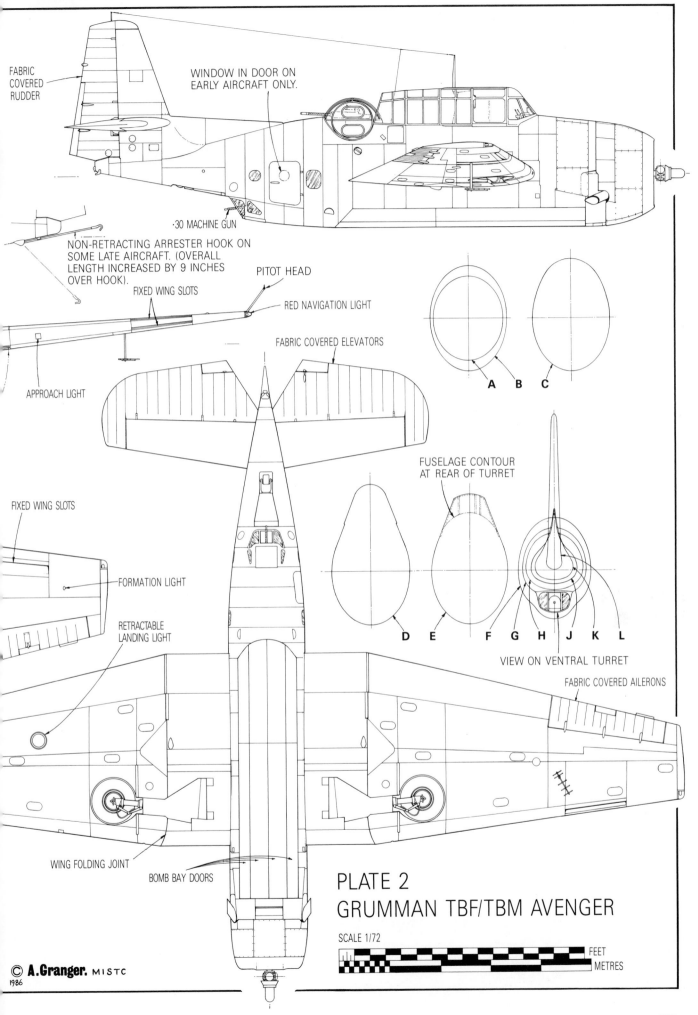

FABRIC
COVERED
RUDDER

WINDOW IN DOOR ON
EARLY AIRCRAFT ONLY.

·30 MACHINE GUN

NON-RETRACTING ARRESTER HOOK ON
SOME LATE AIRCRAFT. (OVERALL
LENGTH INCREASED BY 9 INCHES
OVER HOOK).

FIXED WING SLOTS

PITOT HEAD

RED NAVIGATION LIGHT

APPROACH LIGHT

FABRIC COVERED ELEVATORS

FIXED WING SLOTS

FORMATION LIGHT

RETRACTABLE
LANDING LIGHT

WING FOLDING JOINT

BOMB BAY DOORS

A B   C

FUSELAGE CONTOUR
AT REAR OF TURRET

D   E   F G H J K L

VIEW ON VENTRAL TURRET

FABRIC COVERED AILERONS

PLATE 2
GRUMAN TBF/TBM AVENGER

SCALE 1/72

FEET
METRES

© A. Granger. MISTC
1986

105

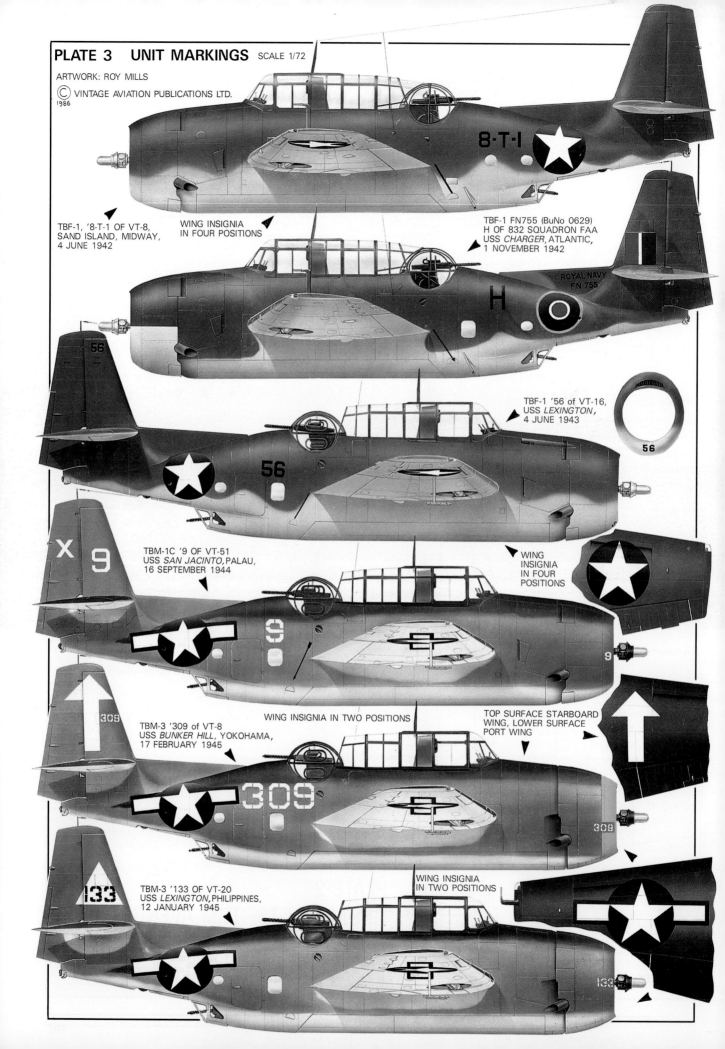

PLATE 3   UNIT MARKINGS SCALE 1/72

ARTWORK: ROY MILLS

© VINTAGE AVIATION PUBLICATIONS LTD.
1986

8-T-1

TBF-1, '8-T-1 OF VT-8,
SAND ISLAND, MIDWAY,
4 JUNE 1942

WING INSIGNIA
IN FOUR POSITIONS

TBF-1 FN755 (BuNo 0629)
H OF 832 SQUADRON FAA
USS *CHARGER*, ATLANTIC,
1 NOVEMBER 1942

ROYAL NAVY
FN 755

H

56

TBF-1 '56 of VT-16,
USS *LEXINGTON*,
4 JUNE 1943

56

56

X 9

TBM-1C '9 OF VT-51
USS *SAN JACINTO*, PALAU,
16 SEPTEMBER 1944

WING
INSIGNIA
IN FOUR
POSITIONS

9

9

309

TBM-3 '309 of VT-8
USS *BUNKER HILL*, YOKOHAMA,
17 FEBRUARY 1945

WING INSIGNIA IN TWO POSITIONS

TOP SURFACE STARBOARD
WING, LOWER SURFACE
PORT WING

309

309

133

TBM-3 '133 OF VT-20
USS *LEXINGTON*, PHILIPPINES,
12 JANUARY 1945

WING INSIGNIA
IN TWO POSITIONS

133

Fig. 15 A TBM-1C of **Monterey's VT-28** *is seen over the advancing invasion fleet off Saipan, June 1944. (USN/NARS)*

The first production TBF-1 and first service test airframe was delivered to NAS Anacostia by the end of January with production and delivery pace picking up quickly. By March, the first combat squadron personnel, 21 aircrews of *Hornet's* VT-8 were assigned to NAS Norfolk for transition into the Avenger. (These aircrew actually made up a second, "parallel", VT-8 because a full squadron by that same name was at the same time on board *Hornet* en route for Pearl Harbor, equipped with TBDs.) In record time, because of the anticipated involvement of their carrier in the Midway Campaign, the 21 crews departed with their new TBF-1s for the West Coast after only a few days familiarisation, then were embarked on an aircraft transport for shipment to Hawaii. Once there, having missed *Hornet*, six crews were detached for forward posting at the Marine base on Sand Island, Midway. They arrived only days before the Japanese attack.

The six-plane detachment of VT-8 was in action at 0600 on 4 June 1942. It was to be an uncharacteristically unsuccessful day for the Avenger. Maybe it was the crew's unfamiliarity with the "Turkey" (the Avenger's most enduring nickname, supposedly derived from the similarity of the two "birds'" appearance in the air). Also a factor was the lack of fighter escort, the Marine Wildcats and Buffalos meeting their own sad fate in a separate engagement. Whatever the cause, the six VT-8 Avengers engaged that day were overwhelmed. Led by Lt Fieberling, they found the Japanese carriers around 0700 and began their attacks immediately. Between the combined effects of the CAP Zeros and effective medium-AA, five out of the six were shot down on the run-in. It is not known how many actually launched torpedos, but no hits were obtained. The surviving TBF-1, "8-T-1", flown by Ens A. K. Earnest, arrived back at Midway completely shot up, hydraulics barely functioning and with the radio operator dead and bombardier wounded. When combined with the toll exacted from the carrier-based, Devastator-equipped section of VT-8 later in the day, the tally reaches suicidal proportions. Of 21 VT-8 aircraft engaged that day, 20 were lost in combat with the enemy. Of 47 crewmen, 44 died. Never in US aviation history, and never since, had a squadron paid such a price, but the results of that decisive battle and the role that the sacrifice of VT-8 played in it, seemed to justify even this extreme cost.

Fig. 16 *A quartet of VT-15 TBF-1Cs off* **Essex** *are seen en route to Guam, 15 July 1944. Note the underwing rocket rails. Also note the tail stripe, the early marking for* **Essex***'s CVG. (USN/NARS)*

Incredibly, VT-8 had not been wiped out of existence. The 16 remaining Avenger crews that had sat out the battle at Ford Island now joined *Saratoga*'s air group and departed, along with *Enterprise* and *Wasp*, for the South Pacific. (Those two carriers now were also Avenger equipped, both VT-3 and VT-7 deploying TBF-1s.) That force arrived in time to lend support to the Guadacanal landings and remained for the expected Japanese reaction. That came on 24 August 1942, when Adm Nagumo led Japan's two remaining Pearl Harbor veterans, *Shokaku* and *Zuikaku*, and the light carrier *Ryujo* against the three American flattops. The Americans found Nagumo's decoy, *Ryujo* in the morning on the 24th, but correctly suspecting a trap, the American Adm Fletcher hesitated attacking the obvious target until 1315, when a 23-plane strike off *Enterprise* (including seven VT-3 TBF-1s) was launched. When another half hour had passed without further enemy sightings and with radar evidence of a strike off *Ryoju* against the Marines on Guadacanal, Fletcher relented and authorised a second, larger, attack of 37 aircraft (including eight VT-8 Avengers) off *Saratoga*. (*Wasp*, imprudently, had been detached for refuelling to the south just before the battle and thus missed the action.) The two waves co-ordinated against *Ryujo* which put up a fierce, if ultimately futile, defence. Only two of VT-3's Avengers found *Ryujo*, neither got a hit and one was shot down. VT-8 was more successful. The eight TBFs obtained at least one hit, finishing the SBD's work, and lost none of their own in the process. In the meanwhile, however, the Japanese big carriers had found *Enterprise*

and holed her, forcing her retirement for repairs. The Battle of the Eastern Solomons was probably the least decisive carrier engagement of the war, but for the Avenger it represented a coming of age. Unlike at Midway, this time TBFs had flown as part of an organised air strike and proved themselves to be an effective replacement for, and improvement over, the Devastator.

Before and after that battle, Henderson Field on Guadacanal served as an emergency base and overnight stop for the carrier-based VTs. It was only on 31 August, when *Saratoga* was again torpedoed by a Japanese submarine, that Henderson received its first "resident" Avengers, a six-plane detachment of the ubiquitous VT-8 under Lt H. H. Larsen. Once there, the TBF-1s became intimately involved in the effort to block the "Tokyo Express", the almost nightly traffic of Japanese destroyers between Rabaul and Guadacanal. The land force of Avengers was reinforced each time there was a disaster at sea (and this period in late 1942 in the South Pacific was easily the most disastrous for the US Navy). When *Wasp* was sunk on 15 September, VT-7 Avengers joined the VT-8 survivors. After the Battle of Santa Cruz on 26 October (in which *Hornet* was sunk and *Enterprise* redamaged), more TBFs came ashore, primarily from *Enterprise*'s VT-10. On 12–13 November, nine VT-10 TBF-1s under Lt J. F. Sutherland finished off the battlecruiser *Hiei* off Savo Island and the next day sank the heavy cruiser *Kinugasa*. Later in November, the first Marine Avenger unit, VMSB-131, arrived at Henderson and the Navy aircrews were rapidly withdrawn.

Fig. 17 Targets in flames below, this VT-51 TBF-1C off San Jacinto makes a final pass over Palau, 16 September 1944. The 'X' on the rudder was CVG-51's marking before the 'G' system was introduced. (USN/NARS)

Fig. 18   A pair of Hancock's Avengers leave a target smoking in the water off the Philippines, 12 January 1945. VT-7 shared CVG-7's 'Omega' insignia. (USN/NARS)

Fig. 19 An Atlantic-based TBM-1C has nosed over on catching the barrier. The two-tone grey ASW Scheme II was adopted for use in the Atlantic theatre in early 1944. The bombardier's hatch can be seen hanging open. (USN)

Fig. 20 A foredeck full of Avenger IIs (TBM-1Cs) is seen on HMS Illustrious, December 1944, Ceylon. The Avenger proved to be very popular with RN pilots, who liked its size and stability. These aircraft would soon be engaged in raids on the East Indies. (US Army)

The Royal Navy accepted its first TBF-1 (BuNo 00616, RAF s/n FN750), which it originally dubbed Tarpon Mk I, in early 1943 at NAS Norfolk. No 832 Squadron finished working up on the TBF by April and deployed on the again repaired *Saratoga* for deployment in support of the landings in the middle Solomons. This particular unit remained in the Pacific, actively engaged in carrier operations against the Japanese, until the end of the war. After its first deployment, however, it operated exclusively off RN carriers, serving successively on *Victorious*, *Illustrious* and *Begum*. Most of the eight other RN Avenger units formed before the end of 1943 were land based being engaged mainly in ASW work in home waters. Except for a few anti-shipping raids in the Channel, most of the RN's Avenger squadrons led relatively uneventful lives. Only those actively engaged in the Pacific, specifically Nos 832 and 834 Squadrons, and later also 820, 848, 849, 854 and 857 Squadrons, saw much combat, flying operations against Surabaya, Palembang, Formosa and the Japanese mainland. Before the end of the war, the Royal Navy would receive 402 Avenger Is (TBF-1s), 334 Avenger IIs (TBM-1/1Cs) and 292 Avenger IIIs (TBM-3s). In all, 15 RN squadrons were equipped with "Turkeys".

During late 1942, the standard TBF-1 was replaced on the Bethpage assembly line by the TBF-1C (the -1B was the official USN designation for the RN Avenger I), identical except for an increase in fixed forward firepower from one to two .50 (12.7mm) machine guns, now fitted one in each wing. At the same time, production began on the TBM-1, the Eastern Aircraft version of the Avenger. Formed from now-idle General Motors assembly plants, Eastern was assigned the task of producing Wildcats and Avengers, freeing Grumman's taxed facilities for the production of the new F6F Hellcat. The transition of production was slow at first, as the differences between the requirements of auto and aircraft manufacture were found to be greater than first suspected. It was mid-1942 before the first TBM-1 was finished, but the pace picked up rapidly. Still, only 550 TBM-1s were finished compared to approximately 1200 TBF-1s (Grumman did not distinguish between -1 and -1C production, so exact figures do not exist). By year's end, however, the Trenton, NJ, final assembly line was going at full speed. 2336 TBM-1Cs were completed as opposed to about 1000 from Bethpage. By summer 1943, Grumman was completely out of the TBF business, all further Avengers being Eastern built.

Grumman's final act in the Avenger story was the design of the XTBF-3. This was preceded by a single XTBF-2, a revised TBF-1 fitted with a 1900hp XR-2600-10. The -3 was identical but substituted a similarly powered R-2600-20. The change in powerplant led directly to the only visible changes from the -1C, an increase in the number of cowl flaps and the addition of an airscoop on the lower cowl lip. The other standard features of -3-series, the provision of an underwing rack for depth charge, small bomb or drop tank and four zero-length rocket rails on each side, were actually introduced during the TBF-1C production run. There were two XTBF-3 prototypes and a further four XTBM-3s, followed by 4657 production TBM-3s.

Avengers served out the war as the standard US Navy carrier-based torpedo/level bomber. But, perhaps even more so than the SB2C, the TBF/TBM found its usefulness gradually diminishing. As the number of enemy warships dwindled, the need for a torpedo bomber disappeared at the same rate. Even in the hands of experienced aircrew and with complete air superiority, torpedo bombing remained the most dangerous (albeit sometimes the most effective) way of attacking warships. Equally, the need for a level bomber decreased as all of the Navy's attack resources were committed increasingly to ground attack/combat support operations using glide-bombing, strafing and rocket attack. All of these roles could be carried out with almost equal precision by any of the aircraft the Navy was then deploying on its carriers. The only advantage of a dedicated attacker was in range with payload. Over short ranges, a Hellcat or Corsair could carry the same load as an Avenger or Helldiver. Thus, despite the many fine characteristics of the Avenger, at war's end the TBF/TMB was very much "odd man out" as far as standard carrier attack was concerned, newer and faster Helldivers replacing it in most VTs (and later VAs).

This was hardly the end of the Avenger in US Navy hands. As if in response to the reduced need for TBF/TBMs as bombers, Avengers began to appear in a myriad of specialised variants during the war and increasingly thereafter. These variants included:

TBF-1D – Night combat version, AN/APS-6 airborne intercept radar carried in a pod faired into the starboard wing leading edge. Also similar TBM-1D and TBM-3D. If converted from a -1C or -3, wing armament was removed. Used as a formation ship for night fighters and as airborne radar picket.

TBF-1E – Similar to -1D except it carried the AN/APS-4 search radar in a pod under the starboard wing and retained all armament. Also TBM-1E and TBM-3E. Postwar, some were updated with advanced radar and designated TBM-3E2.

TBF-1J – A rare variant with cold-weather equipment, mainly de-icer boots on all leading edges and extra heaters. Also TBM-1J and TBM-3J.

TBF-1L – ASW and sea search variant, fitted with retractable searchlight stowed in the bomb bay. Also TBM-1L and TBM-3L.

TBF-1P – Photo reconnaissance version. Also TBM-1P and TBM-3P.

TBM-3H – Early surface search variant.

TBM-3M – A few standard -3s were converted to missile launching configuration. Also a more advanced TBM-3M2.

TBM-3N – Night attack version of the TBM-3.

TBM-3Q – Electronic countermeasures variant with a large ventral radome.

TMB-3R – Ship-to-shore communication variant used during the Korean War. The turret was removed and provision made for upgraded electronics and a crew of seven.

TMB-3S – ASW strike variant, half of the Navy's first "hunter-killer" team. Most were converted from TBM-3E2s.

TBM-3U – A utility conversion, most interior fittings being removed. The US Navy's first COD (Carrier Onboard Delivery) aircraft. It was used extensively during the Korean War for the transport of high-priority cargoes from Japan to the fleet.

TBM-3W – The other half of the "hunter-killer" team, carrying the large APS-20 radar in a ventral radome similar to the -3Q's.

Fig. 21   A TBM-1E test ship sits on the apron at the US Navy's test centre NATC Patuxent River, 31 July 1944. The removable AN/APS-4 pod can be seen under the starboard wing. The last three digits of its Bureau Number (45707) can be seen on its cowling. (USN/NHC)

Fig. 22 A wide yellow stripe across the tail and rudder marks this TBM-3 of Makin Island's VC-84, 9 January 1945. Consistent markings for escort carrier groups, a very complex geometric system, were introduced only in June 1945. The -3's characteristic extended cowl flaps and chin air scoop can be seen. (USN/NARS)

Fig. 23   A VT-45 TBM-3 catches a late wire coming on board **San Jacinto,** *21 March 1945. The white square and black numeral on the tail was that carrier's 'G' marking. (USN/NARS)*

Fig. 24 A pair of TBM-3Es overfly a destroyer during a training flight on 10 March 1950. By this time, the last Avengers were being retired to reserve units. (USN)

In the US and foreign navies, the TBF/TBM served in a myriad of roles until the end of the 1950s, until replaced by specialised aircraft designed for the various tasks Avengers had been modified to perform. Even then it was not done. Its docile nature led to its being extensively employed as a fire bomber, particularly in Canada, well into the 1970s. The US Forest Service at one time had eight. As late as 1969, a total of 66 were registered as water bombers. Rarely has a warplane been able to end its career on such a note. Designed to destroy, the Avenger proved to be such a versatile flying machine that it could end its years in the hands of those trying to preserve.

Fig. 26 A TBM-3W shows off the large ventral radome that housed the APS-20 radar antenna. Note the extra fins added to the stabiliser to offset the loss of stability caused by the radome. (USN)

Fig. 27 A retired TBM-3E (ex-BuNo 91289), now converted to a civilian fire bomber, is seen in the 1950s. (NASM)

SPECIFICATIONS

XTBF-1

Dimensions: length, 40ft 9in (12421mm); span, 54ft 2in (16510mm); height, 13ft 9in (4191mm); wing area, 490sq ft (45.5sq m).
Weights: gross weight, 16,412lb (7444kg); empty weight, 10,555lb (4788kg).
Performance: max speed at 12,000ft (3658m), 271mph (436km/hr); rate of climb, 1430ft/min (436m/min); range, 1125 miles (1811km); ceiling, 22,400ft (6828m).
Powerplant: Wright R-2600-8 Cyclone 14 of 1700hp takeoff power.
Armament: 2×.50 (12.7mm) machine guns (1 fixed, 1 flexible); 1×.30 (7.62mm) flexible machine gun; 4×500lb (227kg) or 1×1000lb (454kg) bomb or 1×Mk XVIII torpedo.

TBF-1C

Dimensions: length, 40ft 9in (12421mm); span, 54ft 2in (16510mm); height, 13ft 9in (4191mm); wing area, 490sq ft (45.5sq m).
Weights: gross weight, 16,412lb (7444kg); empty weight, 10,555lb (4788kg).
Performance: max speed at 12,000ft (3658m), 257mph (414km/hr); rate of climb, 1430ft/min (436m/min); range, 1105 miles (1778km); ceiling, 21,400ft (6523m).
Powerplant: Wright R-2600-8 Cyclone 14 of 1700hp takeoff power.
Armament: 3×.50 (12.7mm) machine guns (2 fixed, 1 flexible); 1×.30 (7.62mm) flexible machine gun; 4×500lb (227kg) or 1×1000lb (454kg) bomb or 1×Mk XVIII torpedo.